Unbridled Grace

A True Story about the Power of Choice

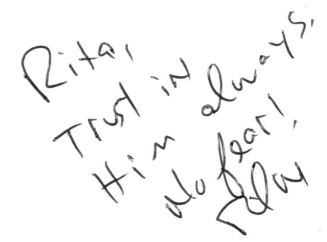

By Dr. Michael J. Norman

First published by Dog Ear Publishing
4010 W. 86th Street, Ste H
Indianapolis, IN 46268
www.dogearpublishing.net

ISBN: 978-145750-096-1
Library of Congress Control Number: 2011926564

This book is printed on acid-free paper.

Printed in the United States of America

To Laura, Madison and Joshua,
I love you very much.

Acknowledgements

It is no mere cliché when it has been said that only in the toughest of times, do we truly learn who our friends are. During our family's six-year nightmare, we were surrounded by many courageous and loving individuals who refused to let us walk alone.

An incredible multitude, too numerous to record, selflessly offered their support and prayers for our family during the darkest of days. Be assured, they were truly felt and kept us going. All of you were light in the darkness and we are forever grateful for your love, support and courage.

I would like to individually acknowledge several others who have greatly helped our family, not only during our ordeal, but also in the years following:

Laura's mother, Dee, and my parents, Joe and Kathleen. Thank you for your continuous support, love and encouragement.

Father John and Jim. I hope these pages do justice to the incredible blessing you both have been for our family.

Suzanne Davis and Maxine Reynolds. Two special family members who left us too soon. You both taught us to face life's difficulties with a wonderful spirit of joy, strength and courage. Your examples remain with us today.

The Consecrated Women of Regnum Christi, particularly of The Highlands School. Your support, guidance, education and prayers provided a safe harbor in the tempest, especially for Madison. For several years, you represented the only area of our lives that remained stable.

A huge thank you to Brenda Grant. Your advice, wisdom and encouragement always seemed to come when we needed it the most.

I want to thank my patients at Norman Chiropractic & Wellness. It is a privilege to serve you. Your trust and belief in the natural, drug-free principles of health and wellness inspire me daily.

Thank you Jim Courtney and the RCIA team at St. Ann's Parish in Coppell, Texas. You greatly helped unite our family in faith and inspired us to continuously go deeper in the study of our faith.

My extreme gratitude to Fr. Thomas Santa, C.Ss. R., Charles Roth, Frank Cunningham and others at the 2007 Catholic Writers Retreat. You took my vague idea for a book and convinced me that it could become a reality.

Thank you to Fr. Stephen Sanchez, O.C.D., for your invaluable advice and direction. You graciously opened the doors of Mt. Carmel Center to me where I spent many hours writing and re-writing in the quiet solitude of your monastery.

Thank you Keith Carroll for reviewing my manuscript and providing tremendous advice and direction at a time when the forest was hopelessly lost because of all those stubborn trees in the way.

Thanks Be to God for giving our family the grace and strength to live up to and become who He knew we could become throughout our ordeal. It was not easy then, just as it is not easy today. Nonetheless, we pick up our crosses and continue to walk.

And finally, I am thankful for the essence of our Christian faith which unites all of us. It's all about the message! (An unwavering trust in the One who came to die for us because of a love we shall never comprehend). May His message always transcend His messengers and serve as an inspiration and reminder to Christians everywhere despite our faith traditions and unique differences.

January 2011

Table of Contents

Introduction

"We make choices every day of our lives. Each choice opens the door to other choices...and for better or worse, our lives are the sum total of our decisions. The little decisions we make today will have a big effect on our tomorrow."

Unknown

I WILL NEVER FORGET THAT feeling I had on Thanksgiving night in 1999. I was thoroughly exhausted and drained. Trying to be somebody you are not will do that to you. I had spent the past ten hours surrounded by loving family and friends on what had always been my favorite holiday. I had tried to enjoy the wonderful helpings of turkey and stuffing and the endless desserts. I had tried desperately to remain present and engaged in the lively conversation and nonstop laughter. And, as a last resort, I had sat down and tried to lose myself in the annual Thanksgiving Day Dallas Cowboys football game in a room full of cheering fans. None of this mattered. I just felt worse and increasingly more alone and isolated. It was as if I occupied a completely different planet than my Thanksgiving dinner counterparts.

After returning to our quiet home that evening, I decided to go for a long walk. I took two things: my border collie, Playdoh, and a new journal I had recently decided to start.

On that cold, wet November evening, our town was eerily quiet and still. Thanksgiving dinner seemed to have claimed everybody for an early bedtime. I easily found the empty park bench I wanted, let Playdoh off her leash to go explore, and opened my journal and began to write.

11/25/99 I have decided to keep a journal of my thoughts during this, my most serious crisis so far in my 32-year life. I hope someday it is of use to some person and it helps them in some way during their crisis.

I begin by first saying, I currently find myself lost within the depths of the pit that I have read about many times in the Bible. It is a pit of darkness, isolation, fear, worry, hopelessness, uncertainty, depression, shame, misery, and evil. In short, my pit has been one in the making since I took a part-time chiropractic job back in November 1994. This job happened to have employers that were members of a Russian organized crime ring involved in money laundering, insurance fraud, and numerous other illegal activities. Only a person with my luck would answer an ad in the paper and be hired by the Mafia!

At present, I find myself under federal indictment. I was arrested at gunpoint by 6 FBI agents after an early-morning raid upon my home 3 months ago on 08/09/99. This occurred in front of my 5-year-old daughter, Madison Elizabeth, who stayed incredibly strong as she sat on the couch watching an episode of "Rug-Rats." While agents in flak jackets and assault weapons stormed through our home, I was slammed up against the wall and handcuffed.

I spent the remainder of the day in the federal jail after being photographed and fingerprinted in the FBI office. What an absolutely degrading and disgraceful ordeal that I wouldn't wish upon anybody. At my arraignment that day as they led me into court, the first two faces I saw were Laura, my wife, and my mother, who looked as if they were going to destroy the FBI agents who were holding me. That brief look upon their faces strengthened me and inspired me in a way I have never experienced. I felt as though I could have broken out of the handcuffs that were clamped tightly around my wrists. Their look is one of the things that keeps me going today.

Currently, my dilemma is one a human being should not have to experience. I have 2 choices before me. Choice #1: Plead guilty to federal perjury, receive probation, avoid prison time, and all additional charges against me will be dropped. However, to receive this "reward," I am expected to "cooperate" with the government. This would mean I would have to lie to put others in prison who I have no knowledge *of wrongdoing. Or, choice #2: Fight this injustice and attempt to do the impossible and risk going to prison for a minimum of 10 years, away from my beautiful wife and 5-year-old daughter.*

Therein lays my dilemma. I have chosen to fight this, and I am currently working with my attorney, the hardest working lawyer I have ever met.

Tonight, I took my dog, Playdoh, my border collie, for a walk, and I prayed to God. I told Him I need help for I am a man without a compass who is very lost right now. Please give me strength, wisdom, courage, and guidance, Father, I pray to you. I cried.

As I read my Thanksgiving journal entry today, I know it falls exceedingly short from conveying the hopelessness and despair from which it was written that night. In our lives, I am convinced, all of us will pass through episodes such as these (if we haven't already), when no one else on earth can come to our rescue. In the end, despite their best intentions, our spouses, children, parents, friends, teachers, pastors, and others can only watch and offer their support. We find ourselves truly alone on our paths, and this mystery of life requires that we alone must take this walk.

In these times of greatest challenge and crisis, I have painfully learned, the true measure of a person is determined. Gold is not forged in the quiet stillness–only through searing heat and grinding metal. Our responsibility becomes to somehow lift ourselves out of the depths of this despair and hopelessness, to somehow discover and choose the path of life God is calling us to walk.

As we look out from these depths in our lives, we are surrounded by an unlimited number of paths, which beckon us with quick promises of freedom and escape from the pain of our ordeals. These paths offer enticing short-term solutions, with many requiring very little effort or sacrifice on our part. At life's most difficult moments, when we are at our lowest and experiencing the greatest amount of pain, the temptation to take these easy paths is almost overwhelming. I vividly remember just wanting the pain to stop without giving much thought to the future.

One other path exists, however, which seems to be set apart from all the rest. You will never find this path too crowded. This is the path of God's will. This higher path is one that initially instills fear deep within our hearts because it requires the greatest sacrifice, possible acceptance of pain, and no promises of easy solutions. Many times, this path of greatest resistance can be viewed as impossible to our limited human intellects.

As we walk upon the road less traveled of bold life choices in accord with God's will, others may see us as foolish, and we definitely will not be understood. If we can muster the strength, boldness, and fearlessness necessary to stay upon this path, however, we find that the greatest of all freedom, happiness, and truth can be ours with the unfolding of some of the greatest blessings of our lives. In the process, we will elevate our destinies and the entire direction of our futures, our families' futures, and the futures of untold others for generations to come.

Our lives are defined by our choices. God's greatest gift to us is our power of choice. He knows the potential we possess and what we can become, and He has given us the way to get there. God's grace is the most powerful force on our planet and can be unleashed by our life choices. Trust Him. This is a story of what God can do with that trust.

The following pages are about hope, encouragement, and inspiration to boldly continue making the life choices that God wants of us. They will never be the easy choices. Whether restoring health, reconciling broken relationships, solving parenting challenges, overcoming self-destructive behaviors, or conquering financial and work stresses, there will always be an initial period of pain and sacrifice if we make the choices God's way; however, as our wills and choices are illumined by the will of God and we embrace our new roles as co-creators, miracles begin to occur. The pain and sacrifice begin to dissipate as we slowly move into the realm of our new creation. In time, we soon discover that our new creation is bigger and better than we could have ever imagined!

The prevailing current coursing through every page of this book repeatedly points us back to the power of choice and God's greatest gift to us; however, several complimentary sub-themes emerged throughout my ordeal and greatly assisted me in transcending significant circumstances. These sub-themes are crucial if we are to consistently elevate and align our powers of choice with the will of God.

The power of choice becomes extremely clear cut as we discover and accept the existence of evil and the spiritual war continuously waged within our world. The story in this book will portray what ordinary evil looks like. Before my experience, I included myself among the millions in our world today who could never have been convinced of an external malevolent force of darkness in our world actively seeking to ruin souls. I was blinded to the spiritual war between good and evil. Sadly, I paid dearly for my ignorance.

Our power of choice is also greatly advanced with an understanding of a second sub-theme emerging within my story. I learned very quickly that bad things happen to good people. Although we will never know what our lives will bring to us, we can be assured that this life experience will bring us face to face with many misfortunes. We must distinguish between the redemptive sufferings that God permits into our lives to bring about a greater good and the self-imposed sufferings as a result of our own poor choices. It remains up to us to choose if suffering is to be meritorious for ourselves and others or if it is to be merely wasted as "pain without a promise." My story possesses a healthy mixture of both.

The boldness of our power of choice is increased further by a third sub-theme as our ideas of family are greatly expanded. My story will introduce many special individuals who courageously stood up for my family and me, becoming lights in the darkness. Additionally, countless many others stood up and joined our fight as well. These were family members of a different sort and not entirely visible to those of us in this life. This occurred when the Mystical Body of Christ, our true family, was revealed. We gain a supernatural strength and resolve to face any difficulty in life as the understanding of our mystical inter-connectedness with all souls, living and dead, begins to grow. (Rom 8:38; 12:5) Nobody can make it alone. Foolishly, for far too long, I tried.

A final sub-theme that surfaces within my story is one that has the potential to absolutely paralyze our power of choice with inaction or completely lead us down the wrong life path altogether because of the human emotions of pride and fear. How do we really know the voice of God and His will for us? How can we distinguish this from our own human will, intellect, and ego? Which voice do we follow? How do we consistently discern and cultivate God's voice in our lives?

For the beginning of this story, and for most of my adult life, these questions kept me shackled in the wilderness. Worse yet, I failed to realize it or even care. My voice and my will were all that mattered. Even though I considered myself a Christian, I was so entrenched in my way of life, it was going to take a major life-altering event to rock my world and change my orientation. This is exactly what God gave me.

On that cold, wet Thanksgiving evening in 1999, I was blind, but now I see. It is now quite obvious that I clearly moved through a deep personal conversion. The conversion of our hearts is permitted and moved along through our power of choice. Our conversions can also be rejected through the same power of choice, stopping the process in its tracks, along with its ensuing accompaniment of graces and blessings. There are many times when my story felt as if I was climbing a mountain—not some triumphal march directly to the peak but rather a host of alternating periods of exhilarating progress with frustrating missteps resulting in considerable falling back. As we climb the mountain of our Christian life, there will always be many ups and downs on the way up.

One pebble can produce the ripple effect on the pond. We can choose to be that pebble. Just as a pebble of greater density and projected with considerable force produces a more profound impact on the tranquil pond, so too, can be our effect as individuals. When we project bold life choices into our world in accordance with God's will and this choice is bolstered with tremendous character, integrity, and purpose, the immensity of our impact can be unimaginable.

Freedom is ours. The future awaits our choices. Our choices will echo for eternity. We have a very short time to make this eternal difference. We can use God's greatest gift to us and choose to be instruments of His grace, the most powerful force on our planet. The life-changing choices we make in accord with God's will, particularly amid the darkness, determine who we are, where we will go, and how we will impact others, now and in the future.

Until now, have you been an effective steward of God's greatest gift to you? What will be the result from your lifetime of choices? How many souls will be touched by your ripple effect? I offer the following pages in hopes of greatly expanding the answers to these questions. Choices today can result in a host of untold miracles for our lives. Even better, good choices today can become a generational family blessing for years to come, affecting souls we may never meet here on Earth!

CHAPTER ONE:

The Search for Naivety

"I don't know what the future holds, but I do know who holds the future."

Rev. Martin Luther King Jr.

Licensed	P/T
Chiropractor	570-5855

FOR YEARS, I WAS PLAGUED by what-if scenarios permeating my mind. What if the deliveryman had forgotten my paper that day? What if I had been too busy to read the paper that day? Why had I surveyed the classified ads that day? Why had that microscopic two-line classified ad so strongly caught my eye back in October 1994? For a time, I guess, you could say I was obsessed with thoughts of how different the next six years of my life would have been if I had simply not found and read that tiny, obscure ad hidden in the paper that day. And to top it off, I would learn that the ad only ran for a couple of days.

I am referring to the tiny classified ad that Irving Healthcare used to attract applicants for employment and that first led me to contact them. I eagerly faxed a copy of my resume the following day and unknowingly set in motion a six-year chain of events that would change my and my family's lives forever.

"This is a gift from God," I remember thinking and telling my wife, Laura, regarding the prospects of a new part-time job for myself. I told her of the tiny classified ad seeking a part-time chiropractic position in the Dallas area. We were excited to think of the additional income and that it would not interfere with my private-practice hours. We thought this had to be an answer to our prayers!

Laura and I had been married two years earlier and were just starting our careers and enjoying a happy start to our marriage. We had first met in high school. In our school of 1500 students, I had been instantly drawn to Laura's beautiful dark eyes and long, dark hair that were products of her French-Indian heritage. Her skin possessed a radiant glow that was shared by all the females within her family. It was as if they had discovered the fountain of youth and this radiance prevented all of them from aging.

Laura's French-Indian features went beyond her outward appearance. The fiery spark in her eyes betrayed the immensity of her soul within, and her compassion for others was stronger than any other I had encountered. From the moment I met her, Laura was always sticking up for the underdog. When she encountered injustice, her temper would emerge as she stood up against bullies of all sizes. This quality compelled her to always speak truth from her heart. In approaching life, Laura led with her heart, even if it meant becoming vulnerable or occasionally being trampled upon by others. Laura never knew a stranger, and I had never met anybody like her.

What I had no way of knowing at the time was exactly where this fire and compassion came from. From the moment she was born, Laura was forced to fight. Born two months premature and losing her twin sister, Elizabeth, at birth, Laura's fight had started early.

The challenges of Laura's childhood continued to forge her personality. Her early family years were characterized by her father's physical and verbal abuse within the home. At a young age, she learned to come to the defense of her mother and younger sister. After her parents' acrimonious divorce, subsequent courtroom battles followed, and Laura grew up amid the struggles of a single-parent home. Laura gained her uncanny strength and independence at a very young age. These characteristics would prove invaluable to all of us many decades later, as the life of our young family would hang in the balance.

We had just recently celebrated the birth of our first child, Madison Elizabeth, eight months before I answered the ad in the paper. Despite dyslexia, Laura had recently fought her way to college graduation with a finance degree. She was the "numbers" person in our family and worked in the payroll and accounting department for a large retail chain in Dallas.

Unlike Laura, I detested everything about numbers. I would prefer a kidney stone to going through college algebra again. I had chosen to become a Doctor of Chiropractic. Chiropractic is a natural approach to health without the use of drugs and surgery. I decided I wanted to help people regain their health and prolong their lives rather than dealing with numbers all day. I had completed my bachelor's degree and attained my Doctorate of Chiropractic in just over six years. I had opened a private family practice in 1992. Laura and I both lived and worked in the same northern Dallas suburb that we had grown up in as kids.

Our true love in life was our daughter. Madison was our miracle. Just like her mother, she was born two months premature and weighed just five and a half pounds. Her fight began early in life also, as she defied all odds of survival.

During her first trimester, Laura had developed a rare health condition. As her pregnancy progressed, her liver and kidneys had begun to fail. Laura's blood pressure also began to skyrocket, putting her in danger of a stroke. The pregnancy essentially would be a race to deliver Madison before her mom's body would give out.

It was during this time that Laura and I learned that we would not be able to have additional children. Doctors advised us that Laura's body would not survive another episode like this one. In fact, we would be extremely lucky if Laura and Madison both survived the current pregnancy.

Laura and I were heartbroken. Our large family would never be. Nonetheless, we decided we would be grateful to God with any size family, if He could just permit all of us to come through this healthy.

Madison's birth weight would have been just two or three pounds if not for another unexpected complication. Laura developed gestational diabetes, which we believe in the end was a Godsend. Although also very dangerous for a mother and her child, a frequent result of this condition is increased weight gain for a baby. These extra pounds would help save Madison's life.

Before Madison's delivery, the doctor pulled me aside and warned me that I may have to make a decision on which life to save, Laura's or Madison's. Laura and I each had different opinions on that choice, and I am thankful it never came down to that. On February 24, 1994, at 5:44 p.m., a delicate, but successful, C-section was performed and our daughter entered the world.

Although the following weeks were filled with intensive care units, incubators, respirators, and every type of medical device imaginable, Madison slowly gained enough weight to come home with us. Laura's body began to slowly recover also. A majority of her damaged organs would heal over time. It was hard to imagine anyone on earth possessing the happiness we had at that time, as our family took on a trinitarian form. After Madison's miracle entrance into this world, we truly felt we had been entrusted with God's special child.

This was the reason we decided Laura would stay home and be a full-time mom. It was an easy decision to make, although a few details had to be worked out. With fresh student loan debt and new business debt, we were barely scraping by even with both of us working. Some tough decisions had to be made, but both of us would willingly do whatever was necessary.

In this period of uncertainty, as Laura was poised to quit her job and enter the world of full-time motherhood, we were looking for some reassuring sign to convince us of the rightness of our decision. It was then, as we cashed in our meager savings account and began practicing our lifestyle of frugality, that I encountered the classified ad in October 1994. For Laura and me, this was the potential answer to our prayers as we moved toward our goal with a focused determination and a machine-like effort of teamwork. We didn't realize then that we would need these cooperative character traits in the not too distant future in a far greater battle.

A few days after faxing in my information, I was interviewed and eventually hired by one of the owners of the clinic, Mr. Lee. I learned he was part owner of the office, along with another man who was currently out of town. A young, friendly Taiwanese businessman, Mr. Lee was looking to duplicate the success of a similar Houston clinic that he had opened a year earlier.

In a trusting, professional, and friendly manner, Mr. Lee promised to turn all medical decision making over to me to free himself up for administrative duties and the recruiting of new business. The center would primarily treat car-accident victims, and my job would be to render chiropractic treatment and therapy modalities to the patients as I supervised their recovery from various injuries.

Mr. Lee raved about the superiority of his staff. They would personally perform most of the therapy and rehabilitation to make my job easier. Additionally, they would act as interpreters for the primarily Spanish-speaking patients he would secure from his marketing efforts. Mr. Lee went on to indicate that my work could be accomplished in a three-day work week, fitting perfectly within my spare time from my existing private practice.

Everything seemed to fall in place, and I was convinced I had found the perfect opportunity. I would be paid $22.50 per hour for my work, with no employment contracts, employee manuals, time cards, probation periods, or training sessions. Nothing! Any request I made would be instantly granted regarding equipment, supplies, and items related to patient care.

This seemingly wealthy and astute businessman offered me a tremendous opportunity and turned the treatment of patients completely over to me with an unbelievable trust and respect that I had never before experienced: nobody looking over my shoulder, nobody counting my hours, and nobody telling me what to do or how to do it. This was a dream opportunity, and I remember thinking that everything was just meant to be.

Looking back now with much embarrassment, I see that the blindness, naivety, and possible stupidity I possessed is glaringly apparent. Looking back on all the perks of this dream job, a cloud of suspicion surfaces and appears obvious. At that time, however, I viewed it as simply wonderful.

In fact, several years later, it was revealed that a young, naïve doctor fresh out of school was just whom they had been seeking to hire. I would later learn that immediately after I left the office that first day upon being hired, Mr. Lee came out of his office, smiling at his three female office staff. "I think we finally found what we were looking for," he remarked.

As I excitedly drove home to Madison and Laura to share the good news, Mr. Lee and his staff laughed among themselves in the empty office. This is how simply it began. This is how it was possible for someone to answer an ad in the paper and unknowingly go to work for the Mafia.

* * *

I vividly recall one experience that occurred on my very first day on the job at the clinic, shortly after I was hired. Unfortunately, I ignored and completely disregarded this experience at the time. Several years later, I would look back on and use this event to guide me during one of the most crucial decisions of my life.

Just ten minutes into my first day on the job, I called a meeting with the office staff to make introductions and discuss expectations and procedures that I wished to implement within the office. As I was sitting at my desk looking across at the three female office staff members I had inherited, an overwhelming feeling of anxiety overtook me.

I began to sweat, my stomach began to contract, my hands grew ice cold, and my heart began to pound out of my chest.

I had an incredibly strong feeling and sense that I needed to immediately get out of that office—not to simply leave the building but to quit on the spot and run as far away from that place as I could. Something within me sensed something terrifying and was trying to tell me in a way unlike anything I had ever before experienced. As if assisted by a mysterious force trying to help me escape, I felt as if I was being lifted up and out of my chair. Something was urging me to jump up and run away.

Never again will I ignore this emotional message. Unfortunately for me, I forced myself to remain seated at my desk. The meeting continued as I took some deep breaths, drank some water, and forced all the emotion back down inside of myself. Although this was difficult, the emotion diminished and faded within a few minutes; I doubt the three girls were aware that anything had occurred.

I have come to learn that this feeling is the voice of a friend deep within human souls and that such a violent reaction occurs when light descends into an extreme darkness. To ignore this voice is to place our souls in great peril. I was being afforded a blatant opportunity to immediately turn back from the road I had set my course on. This was the perfect opportunity to immediately alter the entire course of the next six years of my family's life.

Unfortunately, I ignored my soul's extreme emotional reaction during those brief moments on November 14, 1994. This would conclude a week of poor life choices on my part. The seeds, although small and seemingly inconsequential, had been planted. The moment is almost imperceptible at the time, when a downward spiral in our lives is initiated. A gentle tug of momentum is begun, as we are slowly drawn toward our self-imposed hell on earth.

All From God's Hand

Sometimes our relationship with God can be like waiting in line at the local banking branch drive-thru. As the minutes drag by and we sit unmoving in our line, we begin to notice the many surrounding cars in the lines around us as they swiftly come and go, finishing their transactions and disappearing out into the city to resume their lives. After watching enough, the temptation of impatience and envy finally gets the best of us and we quickly give up on our line by jumping into the swift-moving line of our neighbors'. Not a moment after our act of apparent wisdom is accomplished, our old line begins to suddenly move forward, leaving us to sit idly by and watch.

God's hand is behind all events. In time, all of us come to discover that all of the events of our lives passed through His loving hands first. He is a loving Father who possesses within His being all past, present, and future in a way our finite minds simply cannot grasp in our space-time mortality. For Him, the past, present, and future are all rolled up into one eternal instant.

Within this life, the closest we shall ever come to understanding this reality is experiencing the human emotion of love. Love transcends the finite and opens the door to the infinite. Time slows, and all memory and imagination (past and future) are pushed aside. The emotion of love brings us very close to this eternal instant.

Emanating out of this eternal instant are unique crosses permitted by God meant only for us to carry. If we accept and carry courageously our unique crosses, we shall then receive the sweetness of unique consolations from God also meant just for us. Sometimes just a mere momentary glimpse of Heaven is all we are afforded; nonetheless, His personalized consolations for us are cherished for the rest of our lives.

Sadly, just like when we sit in the bank drive-thru lines, our attention is all too frequently cast on others. As we fall to this temptation of human nature, the sweet consolations of God meant for us begin to elude our grasp. When we go through life "line-jumping," wanting other people's lives and feeling envious of their circumstances, we still receive crosses but they are not ours. They become crosses with no consolation, misery without merit, and pain without promise.

God knows the things He asks of us are hard; however, He asks of us nothing that He has not already experienced: pain, loss, grief, persecution, betrayal, torture, and death. This understanding from a loving Father is why we are given these gifts of consolations as we struggle with our crosses. Savor these sweet periodic gifts in the midst of painful trials. They were chosen just for us. They will come in the most unexpected places at the most unexpected times. Even if one week of pain yields only one hour of consolation, it is worth it. This one hour of sweetness is greater than any other worldly joy and is a sign of the world to come, when we will no longer have the capacity to feel pain and advance its meritorious effects. Most of our world are "line-jumpers" and they miss out.

By a love we cannot comprehend, we were created out of this eternal instant to make a difference with our lives. In far too brief a time, we will be returning to this eternal instant to render a report on our progress. Our unique combination of talents is no mistake. Our purpose is to glorify God and to serve and lift others, by fully expressing these gifts we have been given. (Mk 12:30–31) With such an eternal essence and destiny and the abundant blessing of gifts given to us, we must return the favor by playing hard and living boldly. God doesn't want us to go through life with our feet on the brakes and playing only halfway. A wise teacher once said that to give ourselves to God halfway is to lose out both here and in eternity.

Avoid the line-jumpers. Cherish life and count the manifold blessings. By embracing our circumstances, we transcend them. Help others do the same. If we can strive daily toward this ideal with full expression of our talents, we will not be far from living lives in our Father's eternal instant. When we do, it delights us, delights others, and delights our loving Father. (Is 62:4)

CHAPTER TWO:

Ensnared in Darkness

"At any rate, you will soon find that the justice of Hell is purely realistic, and concerned only with results. Bring us back food, or be food yourself."

C. S. Lewis

I ENJOYED MY PART-TIME CLINIC employment very much. Having just graduated from college, I gained valuable experience in patient care and learned to manage a variety of health conditions that I would not otherwise have been exposed to. I worked full days on Tuesdays and Thursdays and half days on Fridays and Saturdays. This allowed me to balance my schedule along with my fledgling private practice. I had the best of both worlds.

Irving Healthcare was a personal-injury practice, as opposed to my private family practice. A personal-injury practice treats patients primarily who have been involved in auto accidents, with a few work-related accidents. The patients most commonly exhibited pain symptoms within the joints and soft tissues of the neck and back, but various other complaints also surfaced. These injuries are typical in what falls within a mysterious "no-man's land" in modern healthcare called soft-tissue injury.

A soft-tissue injury patient may be released from the emergency room following an accident with all outward signs of normality regarding exams, X-ray findings, lab tests, and other diagnostic indicators. Despite this, the patient remains in a considerable amount of pain. This is the patient many doctors do not want showing up in their offices because they are forced to rely significantly on the patient's subjective description of his or her condition. In other words, there is no proof of injury except the patient's word.

The multibillion-dollar profit-driven insurance industry views these cases with suspicion. Doctors who choose to treat these soft-tissue injuries relying on patient subjectivity can never win. If tests are run to validate a diagnosis, many tests may show up normal and the doctors may then be accused of running up the bill. If physicians choose to forgo patient tests out of respect for cost, they risk a missed diagnosis or having questions of ethics or incompetence raised regarding treatment. This was the unique challenge I faced within my new job.

The office staff of the clinic was a very pleasant aspect of the job. The staff consisted of three Hispanic females in their twenties, two of them sisters. Each of them had previously worked with the owners in Houston before this recent move to Dallas and this new location. They were very friendly and respectful, having a unique dedication to the office. I immediately saw that this job was their highest priority, and they possessed a rare work ethic for their age.

The oldest of the three, Christina, was the office manager and seemed to act as the controlling, motherly influence over the other two. Nothing occurred in the clinic that failed to catch her eye, and she was quick to discipline the other two female staffers when needed. They all spoke Spanish and provided much of the communication to the primarily Spanish-speaking patient population. Although I tried to learn Spanish words and phrases, I was clueless to most of the conversations. The staff and I all got along very well, managing patients, discussing various topics of the day, and occasionally going to lunch together. The girls particularly enjoyed Laura and Madison's frequent visits to the clinic as they came to meet me for lunch.

Today as I look back, I can see that the three girls also maintained a circular air of protectiveness around them, maintaining a subtle distance between themselves and me. Although I deemed them unimportant at the time, various peculiarities existed regarding the staff. Though the girls were always pleasant and friendly, I recall instances of Spanish conversations that nevertheless uncomfortably ceased as I entered the room. I remember muffled private discussions apart from me with the owners, who were included in the girls' circle of protectiveness.

I also recall certain job perks the staff received, such as the use of the owners' luxurious apartment and new car when they were frequently out of town. This was accompanied with paid dinners and after-hours meetings regarding clinic business. The staff also seemed to personally know all the visiting business associates, who flew in to visit the owners behind closed doors. Also, after several months, there were abrupt and unexplained departures by two of the staff members; I never saw or heard from them again. In my mind, I had felt that I had established great relationships and friendships with these female staff members as we worked closely together over eighteen months. In reality, however, I never really knew them at all.

Outwardly, I found the clinic owners just as pleasant and enjoyable as I found the staff. In addition to Mr. Lee, the forty-something Taiwanese owner who hired me, there was another partner in ownership. He was a much older Russian businessman named Yakov. Standing only about five foot two inches, being approximately fifty years old, and speaking with a slow, thick, and heavy Russian accent, Yakov seemed to me to be a friendly and respectful man. Yakov's outwardly gentle demeanor gave the impression that he would be incapable of harming a fly. With his labored English proficiency, Yakov would always extend to me an almost exaggerated politeness and respectfulness. Despite me being his hourly employee and being half his age, he deferred to me on all matters personal and professional. At the time, this gesture was flattering, but now I know it to be a superb job of deception.

Mr. Lee and Yakov would frequently welcome into the office out-of-town guests whom they would introduce to me between patient visits. These professional businessmen were usually casually dressed and typically from the Northeast or California, although foreign visitors from the Russian states would visit as well. After conducting introductions, the owners would usually accompany their visitors back into their private office, where they met behind closed doors. These meetings were always brief, and the guests would always wish me well as they left the clinic to hurriedly catch their departing flights. These businessmen would always be gracious when they saw me, learn all they could about my family and me, and leave with promises of returning soon to Texas. They definitely were welcomed into this circular air of protectiveness inherent within the clinic, but I was clearly an outsider.

Both clinic owners were always quick with a smile and a joke and seemed to sincerely enjoy being in business. They treated me to many lunches at area restaurants and never let me pick up a bill. We laughed and talked about everything from the news to movies, our families, or simply life in the United States. Adding to the entertainment, Yakov would also enjoy a frequent glass of his favorite Russian vodka, not worrying that it was only noontime.

Their business model was an inspiration to me, showing that you could have fun, treat people right, and also make a significant profit at the same time. My bi-monthly paycheck was always on time, with noticeable indications of their appreciation for my service. I even received a Christmas bonus one year from them. They always sincerely inquired about my family, and I even introduced them to my parents on one occasion. I was truly inspired to work harder toward my own goals when I saw the success that these two owners achieved despite being in a foreign country.

I never experienced a problem with the two owners throughout my clinic employment. In fact, I even entertained hopes that my part-time employment with them would lead into bigger opportunities as they expanded their businesses. I remember excitedly telling Laura one day that maybe we should consider moving to Russia for a couple of years if the opportunity was right. My pathetic naivety knew no bounds!

Just as with the clinic staff, as I look back now, I dismissed as unimportant many peculiarities regarding Mr. Lee and Yakov. Both owners had additional homes in other cities and simply kept a spare apartment in Dallas. I was aware they both had multiple businesses, as well. The owners alternated coming into town to visit the clinic for only three days at a time, on one or two occasions per month. Rarely would both be present at once.

Oddly, there was no apparent form of income coming into the office through the mail, which would be common for a medical office. The only regular arrivals were the array of visiting businessmen who would frequently come to the clinic for the closed-door meetings with the owners before quickly returning to the airport. Sadly, all these experiences made no impression on me at the time. I stayed very busy with a heavy patient load and simply shook the hands of the many visiting businessmen who passed through and wished my family and me well.

On Easter Monday 1996, this house of cards that formed my idyllic employment came crashing down. As I was seeing patients in my own private practice, I was served with a subpoena to appear for a deposition in a civil case related to my part-time job at the clinic. This two-day deposition began to reveal who I was really working for. My bosses were not who they appeared to be.

* * *

It was my understanding that this deposition was for civil litigation arising from some of the personal-injury patients treated at the clinic and my help was necessary to settle the cases. After making several frantic calls, I was also assured in advance by the lawyers involved that the proceeding was routine, no big deal, and they simply needed to ask me some questions. Having never received a subpoena before, or participating in any type of deposition, I felt compelled to do so and agreed to help in any way I could.

When I arrived at the downtown high-rise law office for the deposition, I walked into a large conference room and immediately saw more attorneys than I had ever seen in one place before in my life. Without a doubt, this was the most intimidating room I had ever set foot in. With wall-to-wall expensive business suits and the smell of money in the air, I could not help but think about the sad reality of my inability to afford a gallon of milk on the way home.

Many of the lawyers were seated around a massive rectangular table, and many more were standing along the walls of the room. I also noticed at the end of the table a judge seated who seemed to be presiding over the whole affair. As I made my humble entrance into the room, an eerie silence overtook the proceeding as the bustling activity and conversations conspicuously came to a halt. All eyes fell upon me.

I noticed the facial expressions of the attorneys change to wry smirks as if they definitely were aware of something that I was not. This may be likened to the hunter holding back his giddiness as he is about to seize upon helpless prey. Right then, an intelligent human being should have known something was wrong and immediately run out to hire an attorney. Unfortunately, I failed to follow this course and placed myself in a boiling cauldron of water that would soon heat up more than I could have ever imagined. I had no idea what a deposition should be like and so remained in the room.

I took my seat at the table, and the attorneys began to ask me questions. The questions were easy at first, but then things began to change. One by one, the attorneys began to present evidence to me that the clinic I worked in was more than what it seemed. The evidence indicated that the clinic was actually a front for the Russian Mafia, which had been moving through the North Texas area at that time.

The attorneys showed me evidence that the clinic's address was a shell for multiple other illegal operations. In addition to the medical office, the owners operated a construction company, a textile company doing business in Taiwan, a modular home company doing business in Russia, and established connections to a chain of check-cashing outlets that were helpful in their money-laundering operations.

The only seemingly legitimate operation, the medical clinic, was also surrounded by the tentacles of organized crime. Through an intricate, complex, and secretive network of lawyers, business professionals, and criminals, the Russian Mafia was committing insurance fraud and staging automobile accidents. As I worked for my modest hourly wage, I was shown, the owners were raking in millions of dollars. I seemed to be the only person unaware of what was occurring. Looking back now, I see that I had turned out to be the perfect employee for the Russian Mafia. They were very good at what they did, and in me, they had found just what they were looking for.

I was already feeling sick, then the attorneys showed me something that truly scared the life out of me. As the primary doctor at the clinic, my name and signature appeared throughout all of the illegal documents and evidence being shown to me. Not only medical documents but also their shell corporations prominently displayed my name. They even listed my name on ownership documents, showing me as part owner of their illegal corporations!

My anxiety heightened as I learned more about my employers. I was informed that the Taiwanese owner, Mr. Lee, was a member of one of the wealthiest and most influentially powerful families in Taiwan. In addition, I learned that my other boss, Yakov, the seemingly gentle Russian owner who had shown me nothing but kindness, was connected to a Russian Mafia faction—a faction that, *up until then*, had shown no proclivity toward violence. Getting sicker by the moment, the attorneys then attempted to reassure me. They explained that all the known violence, murder, and drug activity were attributed only to their Russian *friends*. These were the same friends whom I had met continually passing through the clinic!

Just like on my first day at the clinic, I wanted desperately to jump up and run as far away from that deposition as I could. I felt that familiar sharp pain in my stomach again as it wrenched into knots. I struggled to pull a breath from my lungs but felt as if I was suffocating from extreme fear.

Somehow, I managed to complete the deposition as I assured the lawyers repeatedly of my innocence. The lawyers implied that my cause would be greatly helped in their eyes if I could return to the clinic and retrieve evidence for their case. Although I had never possessed a key to the clinic and had very little hope of success, I told them I would try. After that day, however, everything was different. My family and I were now firmly in danger. Upon leaving the law office, I phoned Christina, the clinic office manager.

"Christina, the insurance companies are saying Yakov and Mr. Lee are doing something illegal. I'm quitting. You need to transfer all the patients to another doctor."

"Yakov has been calling here all day to see if I heard how it went. He wants to meet with you right away," she said.

"I can't right now," I said, ending our call with my heart pounding out of my chest. She continued calling me back, but I did not answer.

As I drove home that day, I was forced to pull over into a parking lot, where I threw up.

My family and I were now very vulnerable. I had just been threatened by an army of insurance company lawyers and was being targeted in their multimillion-dollar civil litigation case that would utterly destroy our lives. I knew these people viewed me as a suspect and there was no escaping. In addition, I had discovered extensive information about my Russian Mafia employers, and those employers would soon find out that I knew. And worse yet, I had just testified and volunteered all my support against the Russian Mafia to individuals who were completely indifferent to my plight and powerless to protect me or my family! All that remained to do that day was to go home and collapse into an agonizing paralysis of fear.

At times such as these, options and choices within our lives appear to become very limited as we descend into deep, dark pits of misery. We become swallowed up by the darkness and lose sight of the tiny sliver of light coming down from above. At times when our entire futures are awaiting the choices we make during these periods of crisis, all too often, extreme pain and fear influence us into making inferior choices. Our choices in the dark fail to propel ourselves out of the crisis and toward a higher future. We simply continue our descent.

I was no different, and the poor choices I had made that had led me to my self-imposed hell were only compounded by further bad choices. The light of life for me at this time was growing dim, and I felt enveloped by a heavy interior darkness. I proved to be no match for this, and my naivety clearly continued to conceal what I was truly up against. My enemy, as well as the true nature of evil, was still unknown to me. I was an easy target for this orchestrated, conscious force of ill will directed by something beyond our understanding that prowls the earth, seeking to dim and destroy the vulnerable, faithless, and foundationless and their accompanying assortment of poor life choices.

I stood utterly alone with no place to go. For a time, I was afraid to leave the house. When I did, I remained extremely alert of my surroundings. I spent sleepless nights with one eye open and a firearm within reach.

For someone who always attempted to control life, I was fast being stripped of all control. I attempted to muster my last remaining bastion of human strength needed to seek out a human solution to this nightmare. Instead of mustering the necessary strength and courage and rising to the occasion of this crisis, however, I found myself hopelessly descending further and further into the painful depths of despair and fear. I had become ensnared, and the powerful tentacles of evil were squeezing and constricting their way into our once-tranquil lives. Little could I have imagined that this storm would soon grow much darker with a phone call from the federal government.

Know Thy Enemy

It has been wisely said that the devil's deepest wile against humankind is to persuade us that he does not exist. By so doing, the malevolent force of evil can retreat out of sight and avoid the sanitizing rays of Light that expose all truth. Hidden in the dark recesses and corners of existence, evil can then unleash and orchestrate its deception and manipulation from afar, appealing to a frail and fallen human nature and ruining souls by the millions.

In any battle, success is possible only after learning about the enemy we will be engaging. To go into this battle blind and ill-prepared is to put our power of choice under the devil's influence. We must learn the tendencies, motives, characteristics, weapons, and weaknesses of this enemy if we are to achieve victory. Above all, we must learn to instantly recognize the Kingdom of Darkness in all its deceptive disguises when we are confronted by it and must train our daily power of choice to almost subconsciously side with the Kingdom of Light. Then and only then can the battlefield be tipped in our favor.

To our human understanding, evil shall always remain a puzzling, self-contradictory enigma that can never be reduced to a single factor. Evil's deceptive essence avoids detection by constantly alternating among three distinct natures, much like the con artist's shell game on the street corner.

The first nature of evil existing in our world takes on the form of personal sin. As soon as we are born, the fallen human state and its tendency toward disordered immoral appetites falls prey to evil's enticements to appease our tendencies. Our society fails to understand, and even mocks, the notion of our natural inclination to sensuality, pride, vanity, self-centeredness, envy, and fear. Because of this lack of understanding, we become defenseless to our enemy by not taking on the necessary mortifications that consistently train the flesh away from our appetites.

A second nature that evil uses to cloak itself is the structure of sin. Organizations, coalitions, governments, systems, philosophies of thought, corporations, associations, and others can all easily fall prey to the penetrating tentacles of evil that quickly begin to guide and manipulate the structures to serve its own ends. The self-contradicting and puzzling enigma of evil is further complicated as we find these structures consisting of good, well-meaning, and well-intentioned people who unknowingly become instruments of evil's intentions.

This must not stop us from consistently shedding light on the underlying purposes of these structures, such as greed, power, domination, exploitation, and opposition to truth, to name a few. In response, the structures' enticing message to the populace is always the same. They falsely propose a harmless life of comfort, ease, pleasure, pride, and vanity to an eagerly accepting throng.

A third nature of evil comes in the form of the devil, or Satan himself. Shifting among his trifold nature, this conscious, personal, malevolent entity is real and knows he has but a short time. Because he cannot kill us, he wants us to kill ourselves by driving us to despair, using all possible means. Primarily through fear and deception, the devil preys upon our frail human nature as the lines become confusingly blurred between right and wrong, good and evil, and truth and falsehood.

Satan is the perennial loser, always mad at himself, never happy and never satisfied. He hates himself more than he hates us. His primary weapon against us is fear, and his twisted deceptions toward us are endless. His power over us is greatly broken when we personally defeat and conquer our fears. Without fear, he is left without his greatest weapon and exhibits his fundamental cowardice by backing down from a strong fight.

We must respect Satan's power, but there is no reason to fear him at any time. He is not all-knowing and does not know what we will do next. He slowly learns about us and alters his attacks accordingly. As he discovers and learns of our weaknesses, his temptations to us get more refined with time.

Our weapons against the devil are many, and we should enlist all of them on this spiritual battlefield. Prayer, fasting, charity, redemptive suffering, frequent confession, and reception of the Holy Eucharist are some of the most effective weapons in defeating the three natures of evil, ushering in the Light of God, and illuminating the darkest corners of our world.

In addition to these instruments of holiness, we also have access to one more effective weapon in our arsenal that painfully cuts through Satan's prideful nature like a salted razor blade. Once at the top of the nine levels of angels, Lucifer and the fallen angels now find themselves on the bottom of the angelic hierarchy, forced to look upward at the Queen of all Angels. (Rev 12:1) Satan and his angels hate the Blessed Mother and are repulsed by the idea of a human holding dominion over them. Our prayers for our Lady's intercession in the battle against Satan are extremely effective and powerful, further tipping the battlefield in our favor and crushing the head of the serpent. (Gen 3:15)

Satan does not want us to remember whom we belong to. When we do remember, we know that anything is possible with our lives. Mary is there to remind us. Christ's mother, also our mother, can be found atop this hierarchy, clothed in the radiance of her Son. She freely offers intercession to all of us and imparts to us only one simple command: *Do whatever He tells you.* (Jn. 2:5)

CHAPTER THREE:

Brokenness and Nakedness

"Out of the depths I cry to you, O Lord!"

Psalm 130:1 (NIV)

OVER THE NEXT FEW WEEKS following my insurance company deposition, my fear for my family and myself continued. Each time I left my home or practice, I would check to see if any suspicious cars were parked outside waiting for me. Even so, I still maintained a faint flicker of hope that all of this would blow over.

As I had promised the attorneys, I made plans for one final visit to the medical clinic under the guise of transferring the patients' paperwork out of my care. When I was certain the owners would not be present, I went back. This was a very tense two hours of work. The owners could have walked in at any moment. I had no choice, however, with the threat of the multimillion-dollar civil suit hanging over Laura and me.

As I worked on the patient files and the receptionist was not looking, I gathered what evidence I could. I loaded these items, consisting mainly of copied rolodexes and patient lists, in my backpack then left that office forever.

The insurance company attorneys called me a short time later, and we met at their prearranged location. It felt like a scene out of a spy novel. I handed everything I had over to them. They seemed to convey an appreciation toward me, and for a while I thought maybe this was all over.

These naïve and misguided hopes were dashed just before Christmas, as I was treating patients one day at my private practice.

In front of a startled reception room, the county constable walked in and served me with a federal subpoena. The familiar sharp pain returned as my stomach immediately knotted and I was handed an attachment of ten pages of paper with a ten-dollar bill. The money, I later learned, was a subpoena fee. At the time, however, I thought it was a consolation prize to people who'd had the life scared out of them.

I learned from the attorneys listed on the subpoena that I was being summoned to appear at a federal sentencing hearing for one of the Russian Mafia members. I was reassured by the attorneys that this was a routine matter and my assistance would help greatly in my overall case. With an absolute lack of any money for my own lawyer and my continued insistence that I had done nothing wrong, I again relied totally on the legal advice of these attorneys. What I didn't realize at the time, and what I naively failed to understand, was the fact that I was being called by the defense. Effectively, I was being asked to *assist* the case of the Russian Mafia member against the federal government!

As I walked into the federal courtroom that day, it appeared that the proceedings were in a brief recess. A huddle of people gathered behind the federal prosecutor's table. Quite obviously, these were federal agents of various kinds. They were joined by many of the insurance company attorneys whom I had met at the deposition six months earlier.

I then saw a face that was very familiar to me but whose presence in the courtroom defied all rational explanation in my nightmarish story. As I went up to shake Fred's hand, I could not imagine why the gentle, elderly storage facility manager for my personal storage unit was in that courtroom. Although my naïve, poor choices were predominantly to blame for my current predicament, the ordeal was now expanding far beyond that. The circumstances surrounding this event would later prove to me that my destiny was somehow being led and inextricably enmeshed within this nightmare of an ordeal. At this point, there was seemingly very little I could do to halt the unfolding of these events.

I would later learn that prior to this event in late 1996, the United States Secret Service made an amazing discovery that would be related to my case. A Secret Service Agent named Donaldson was credited with the find that later brought him several awards and accommodations by the agency. He had discovered close to $300,000 cash in an otherwise empty ten–foot-by-ten–foot storage unit after receiving a call from Fred, the storage facility manager.

This cash was stuffed into a very large suitcase and conspicuously set in the middle of the floor of the empty unit. When I later saw several pictures of this empty storage unit with its single suitcase, I thought the suitcase looked as though it could have been filled with explosives instead of the mountain of cash in small-to medium-sized denominations. This discovery was later connected to a Russian organized crime figure who was using this storage unit to assist his money-laundering activities. This is where the story ceases to make sense in terms of my relationship to it.

The discovered storage unit was located in Carrollton, Texas, a northern suburb of Dallas and miles away from any of the Russian business entities. My home and private practice were also located in Carrollton. In addition, Laura and I had also been renting a storage unit in this very same facility. In fact, our specific unit was located almost directly next to the Russian's unit! Although I had never witnessed anything or anybody suspicious at my storage facility, it did not matter. Government agents do not believe in coincidence.

The situation was further compounded by the friendship I had forged with Fred, the friendly, talkative manager at the storage facility. As a long-term tenant, I had gotten to know Fred well. When I visited his facility to pay my rent or retrieve an item from storage, we enjoyed speaking about the topics of the day and other small talk. Aware that I had a private practice right down the street, Fred would frequently turn our conversations to health issues or advice.

Upon entering the courtroom that day, I realized that this friendship brought me further under the government's powerful microscope. As I walked into the courtroom and down the aisle, I was surprised to spot Fred sitting in an aisle seat.

"Hey, Dr. Norman! How are you doing?" he said with his familiar northern accent as he excitedly jumped up and shook my hand.

Almost immediately, I felt the entire first two rows of government agents drop everything they were doing and turn around. They wanted to know who I was. Furthermore, they wanted to know why I was so familiar with their star government witness in their money-laundering case.

My standing with these government agents would be further harmed beyond repair by my next move. I still had to honor my responsibility to the subpoena I was under. I had been advised earlier that it was a criminal charge to not honor that responsibility. I felt I had to testify, so that is exactly what I did.

Unwise life choices on my part had certainly caused this door of darkness to open in my life. With the uncontrollable power of a developing cyclone, however, the momentum of my downward spiral was taking on a life of its own. From that point forward, all rational explanation to the unfolding events of my ordeal were out the window as things began to accelerate. It later became obvious that other forces were at work here, those of darkness and those of light. Just the fact that these Russian organized crime figures with contacts all over the world would pick a storage unit in my hometown, just a few doors away from mine, to base their money-laundering operations convinced me of this.

This is where the unwise use of the power of choice can lead. Even if the choices are initially very small or seemingly inconsequential, we eventually come to a place where we are controlled by others. We cease having control over our own destinies. What a horrible feeling. Like a feather being blown within this raging cyclone, I was now firmly entrenched in this struggle. On my own, I could not free myself from it.

Following my two minutes of courtroom testimony that day, as I naively and unknowingly assisted the Mafia against the federal government, I would soon feel the wrath of the good guys too. Sitting at the federal prosecutors' table, quietly seething inside over my actions, was Assistant U.S. Attorney Hill. I was now his prey and squarely on his radar screen. Over the next several months, I would become the recipient of his targeted vengeance as he set out to utterly dismantle my life.

I staggered out of the courtroom that day in what could best be described as a fog. Somehow, I found my way onto the nearest elevator. Just as the doors were closing, I was joined by two of Hill's henchmen. FBI Agent Stone and IRS Agent Hennessey "asked" if they could meet soon with me to discuss my employers.

* * *

I was reading a children's book with Madison at our local library when I received a page from IRS criminal investigator Hennessey. His demeanor seemed different now from after my courtroom appearance. Right from the start of our phone call, this young, friendly agent formed an immediate and convincing bond with me. He immediately reassured me of his belief of the obvious fact of my innocence and noninvolvement with the Russian Mafia and all of their criminal enterprises. He convinced me of the urgency of our meeting as well as my assistance to him so he could quickly go after these criminals. He was good, almost making me feel as if it was my patriotic duty to help him. Although I didn't quite know this just yet, I was surrounded by deception on all sides and nothing in my life was real anymore.

The meeting was held at the Dallas Secret Service headquarters between myself, IRS Agent Hennessey, and Secret Service Agent Donaldson, the same agent who had discovered the storage unit cash. I entered the maximum-security offices and was led through door after door until I reached the interior of the building. This windowless fortress made me feel as if I was entering a tomb. I am quite sure we would have survived a nuclear war if one had occurred that day. Once again, I was present without an attorney, feeling fully reassured in doing my duty, along with the obvious fact of my innocence; however, I soon was greatly overmatched by what I later learned to be an interrogation technique called "good cop, bad cop."

The first thing I noticed within that tomb was the conspicuous absence of anything alive or anything portrayed to be alive. With no plants, no trees, no fish aquarium, no pictures on the wall, and no windows to the outside world, the room conveyed a sense of death to the subconscious. After being introduced to the two federal agents, however, I realized it was not death they wished to convey, but ultimate human power. For me, this failed miserably, as I still saw death itself.

Agent Hennessey was the first to be in the room with me. Just as he had earlier on the phone, he continued to reassure me and thank me for coming in. We briefly engaged in small talk regarding news and sporting events, and he carefully listened to every word I said. He then informed me that another agent, a Secret Service agent, would be joining us shortly.

"You'll have to excuse him, because sometimes he gets a little overbearing. Don't worry, that's just his nature," he said, almost preparing me like an old friend.

Despite Agent Hennessey's attempts at friendliness, there was nothing endearing about him. When I first met him, he struck me as an extremely odd individual, which made him hard to forget. He seemed to hold a constant smirk on his face, similar to ones the insurance company attorneys in my deposition had worn. What oddly accentuated Agent Hennessey's facial expression, however, was his chin. He had very little of any kind of a chin, with a weak and nondescript bone structure from his lower lip down. This facial abnormality seemed to make his perpetual smirk even more sinister and twisted, instantly leading me to distrust anything and everything about him. Agent Hennessey's odd appearance and smirk betrayed his friendly guise. He gave off the transparent look of a self-aware deceiver who cannot keep a straight face in light of the preposterousness of his assertions.

After what was surely a planned delayed entrance, we were finally joined by Secret Service Agent Donaldson. He was a huge, muscular figure who towered over the smaller IRS agent. He seemed to radiate a darkness out of his heart that was more unnerving than anything I had experienced with the Russian Mafia members. Agent Donaldson firmly shook my hand and quickly conveyed his impatience with me and my criminal involvement with the Russians.

"Look, you need to level with us and tell us the truth about your activities. You're in deep trouble, and you need to make it easier on yourself. You know, you're going to look real good wearing one of those orange jumpsuits," Agent Donaldson said with a laugh, referring to the jail attire.

With the friendly IRS agent seemingly trying to befriend and protect me against the bullying, intimidating Secret Service agent, I still managed to affirm my innocence and answer every question truthfully and to the best of my knowledge. I would later learn that just a couple of years before this meeting, Agent Hennessey had worked for a rental car agency. Now, instead of renting cars, his new powerful position in the federal government, permitted him to hold the very freedom and life of human beings within his grasp. Based on this interview, his interpretation alone would decide my freedom or incarceration.

Unfortunately for me, my answers to their questions were already determined before I ever entered that room. Agent Hennessey decided that what he heard from me in that room equated to a full confession to being a member of the Russian Mafia conspiracy. Nothing I said would have altered his theoretical version of events, least of all, the truth.

* * *

For me, May 1, 1997, was the most difficult and painful day of the entire six-year ordeal. On that day, I was napping soundly with three-year-old Madison. When I awoke, I vaguely remembered our phone ringing and being answered by Laura. Sure enough, a phone message awaited me on the counter. As I read it, the all-too-familiar sickening fear once again came over me as my heart began to beat out of my chest.

The message was from Agent Hennessey, who, I had last seen three weeks before, at our interview. Laura also understood the gravity of this call and was standing next to me. She explained how he had asked for me and how she had told him I was asleep with our daughter. In a rare act of decency for Hennessey, when Laura asked if she should wake me, he had told her to let me sleep.

I called the number, and the agent answered right away. He began to talk to me in the manner that he had used from day one. He always spoke to me apologetically, as if we were friends and he was firmly on my side throughout the ordeal. He first thanked me considerably for my assistance and cooperation and told me he could not have concluded his investigation without me. My slight glimmer of hope was soon dashed when he said, "However, Dr. Norman..." I knew bad news would follow.

"The U.S. Attorney's office has considered your assistance and cooperation, particularly within your interview three weeks ago. They greatly appreciate it. But they just could not justify leaving you out of the federal indictment, which will be coming down soon."

He told me that a great deal of this decision rested in the hands of the lead federal prosecutor, U.S. Attorney Hill, whom I had unknowingly testified against and angered in that sentencing hearing five months before. Agent Hennessey told me that I should expect to be indicted in two weeks and to face a lengthy stay in prison when convicted. After pleading my innocence again to him, he coldly ended the call by giving me U.S. Attorney Hill's phone number.

Naïve to the very end, the next call I immediately made was to Hill. I remained thoroughly convinced that if I could just explain the situation and reason sensibly with these people, all could be quickly straightened out. After making this call to Hill, however, I no longer had that illusion. I remember telling him that I did not want to be arrested. His response to that gave me an ice-cold chill down my spine.

His wrath now very apparent, he calmly but arrogantly replied, "I think we can work something out. Why don't you come on down here to the office, where we could talk it over?"

I thanked him and told him that I first would be contacting an attorney. After I hung up, it felt as if the devil himself had just extended me an invitation to hell to discuss the remainder of my life— a life which was seemingly and completely in his hands at that moment.

After that call, I collapsed onto my living room couch and spent the next two days summoning the strength to simply watch the ceiling fan rotate above me. I was dead to this world on May 1, 1997, and my life was over at that point. Thankfully, Laura's fighting instincts went into high gear for me during those few days. She made an endless number of frantic calls to attorneys all over our city. We were further demoralized by their responses. They repeatedly refused our case and tried to convince her of the absolute hopelessness of our situation. I viewed all of this activity as pointless, however. As the hours passed, an enticing voice emerged from out of the darker corners of my mind and continued to get louder and louder. Its sinister refrain echoed over and over: *There is only one way out of this nightmare.*

A few days later, I was in a downtown law office, trying to get an attorney to take pity on us and accept our case. As I was left alone in a high-rise conference room, I walked over to the plate-glass window and looked down at the street below. I was convinced that I had only one way out.

My existence then was no more than a mere fragile stupor. At that time, I believe, I was clearly out of my mind. My mental state could only be described as a dark psychosis. I was firmly in a tunnel of depression, where the voices and activities of everyday life are muffled and the only point of focus is unshakable mental anguish. *Death is preferable to this*, I thought. I justified that I, along with everybody around me, would be better off without this pathetic specimen of humanity I had become.

I am thankful that I was so weak at that time that I could not even muster the strength and courage to carry through with this plan. I am not proud of who I was during those dark and miserable days. Little did I know then that instead of two weeks, it would be another twenty-eight months before my impending federal criminal indictment would materialize. Fortunately for me and my family, by the end of this period, I would be a completely different person.

The Courage of Humble Submission

Sometimes we forget that God has dreams too. Our destinies are simply God's dreams for us and are bigger than we could ever imagine—so big, in fact, that a great divide separates the people God wants us to become from the people we are currently. As we grow and advance toward this new reality, we shall know no greater happiness; however, we also must accept and experience pain as part of this process. This is the only way to get there. This is also why God *slowly* guides us toward His dreams for us, greatly respecting our free will.

The enemies of our destinies and of God's dreams for us shall always be fear and pride. Nothing else is as insidious and dangerous for the human soul than these traits. Fear and pride blind us to the truth and cause us to turn away from a loving Father who only wants to fulfill all of our desires. An entire human race, meant to ascend and soar upon the wings of eagles, has largely been neutralized and kept from its mission because of fear and pride and Satan's effective use of these instruments.

Our pride shall never go willingly. It is rooted into the very being of our fallen human nature. Since the dawning of existence, we have heard its misleading echo. Our pride views humble submission and surrender to God as a weakness.

Through the blindness and stubbornness of pride, we can become hopelessly entrenched within this deception of self-centered existence. We become incapable or fail to see the need of altering our course, even sometimes believing we are serving God's purposes faithfully. Sadly, we can remain in our presumptuous contentment for many years. There comes a point, however, when others begin to be harmed by our failure to surrender our pride. Refuse to be the pilot flying a jumbo jet full of passengers at night who rebuffs any submission and obedience to the ludicrous, dogmatic authority of runway lights!

This state becomes the occasion where a loving Father allows His children to experience the circumstances that are necessary to root out and destroy the remnants of selfish pride so injurious to ourselves and others. Many times, we have strayed so far off course that we curse the heat of this furnace and fail to believe our Father when He tells us this heat shall usher forth the essence of glittering gold within us.

In humble submission to our Father, these events, finally and thankfully, bring us to our irreverent knees and remind us of our humanness and desire and need for God. As the crucibles of our trials force us to throw off the useless mantles we used to take courage in, we can cry out to our Father with humility in a language the world cannot understand, "You have broken me, Father, but have filled me with love. Thank you."

Surrender, detachment, meekness, and humble submission to God's will is the only path to our destiny and God's dreams for us. Freedom by submission—this is the way we become who we were meant to become. This is the only way to grow and to span the great divide as we become God's new creation. Our first birth involved pain. So also shall our second birth.

Freedom by submission—what a strange paradox. Along with the pain of growing into God's new creation, we also find the freedom and happiness so elusive for so many in this life. The fears of our lives are conquered as we discover a new-found peace and confidence to all that life presents. Nothing disturbs us as we now know exactly who we are in front of a loving Father. We have learned how to react to the inevitable crosses in this life from our Lord, who came into this world to be nailed to a tree rather than exalted, praised, and honored by men as a victorious, conquering recipient of worship. What was our Lord's reaction? Submission, forgiveness, and love. (Lk 23:34)

Our world is in desperate need of courage. There shall never be a greater show of courage than someone who surrenders in humble submission to God's will and love for others, allowing a new creation to usher forth. This is heroic. God is anxious to heal us, but we must first let go to be healed, not the other way around. Where there is no faith, there will be no healing.

We need courage to step forward with our spiritual lives and refuse to be silenced. We need courage to have the submission and humility to cry out to Christ and not worry about what others think of us. And, finally, we need courage to accept and answer the hard and difficult tasks Christ asks of us and become the people we are meant to become.

CHAPTER FOUR:

The Ascent Begins

"O human race! Born to ascend on wings, why do ye fall at such a little wind?"

Dante

IN REGARD TO MY CRIMINAL indictment, the prosecutors exacted a calculated measure of cruelty on me that made my Russian Mafia employers appear to be the good guys. Although I was initially told in the phone call on May 1 to expect an indictment in two weeks, the federal criminal indictment was not issued against me for twenty-eight months. I later learned that this tactic is used to emotionally *break* a defendant by keeping his or her life in such limbo that a guilty plea can be easily procured. This is the fate of 94% of all federal defendants today. The extreme emotional stress soon takes its toll on any individual. Sound judgment is usually replaced by rash, emotional decision making in an effort to escape the pain.

This was where I and my family found ourselves at this time. The time was marked by incredible stress, anxiety, and uncertainty and a painful inability to see or make any type of plans for our future. These paralytic feelings of fear and anxiety were inescapable, as each day was potentially my last. Making it worse, I began to isolate myself because of fear. I missed such important family events as my brother's wedding and my grandfather's funeral.

For the initial few months, as I left my house in the mornings, I would first look up and down the street to see if anyone was waiting. Or I would wonder, *Will today be the day?* I would leave a restaurant with family and friends who were engaged in laughing and conversation, and

I would be miles away, intently focused on the parking lot and any potential government agents awaiting me. It was a miserable time. My head was placed firmly in the guillotine, but my executioners torturously refused to drop the blade for twenty-eight months.

Although Laura still possessed her fighting spirit, she was well aware that she would not be the one in the line of fire. Lovingly, she told me where she stood, and I have always remembered this. "Whatever you decide, I'll do. If you want to run, I'll run. If you want to fight, I'll fight. If you want to plead guilty, that's okay too. I totally understand."

The feeling of paralysis induced by this waiting is something that can easily drive someone into self-destruction. I can see how many people choose to escape this painful state through drugs, alcohol, or something even worse. The consequences of these choices eventually turn truly tragic, however, harming others through divorce, abuse, child neglect, violence, crime, and more. In the end, by taking the road of self-destruction, we never really succeed in escaping or out-running the initial source of pain; instead, we are left with compounded tragedy. Worse, we slam the door on the possibility of God's miracles coming into our lives and on some of life's greatest opportunities for growth.

By avoiding this tempting self-destructive path, an interesting phenomenon started to occur for me. Each day that my head remained in that guillotine without the government dropping the blade, I seemed to grow stronger and more prepared rather than growing weaker and descending the path of self-destruction. This is precisely how suffering becomes a gift. If we allow them to, the painfully hot flames begin to forge and shape us into new creations. I now see that my agonizing twenty-eight months of limbo were also some of the greatest months of my life. Although back then, I did not see it quite so clearly.

After the first few weeks of this period, it became pretty obvious that no one was coming to our rescue. After a frenzied letter-writing campaign to local Congress members, senators, various legal defense organizations, and the ACLU, we received nothing. These protectors of liberty replied only with countless form letters. After touting the merits of their past efforts and their unwavering commitment to service and justice, each reply ended with a courteous explanation about why they could not assist us.

In coming to the realization that no one was going to help, and in time, I slowly began to shake my paralysis and get up off my couch.

I developed a new-found thirst for reading. I set out devouring hundreds of books, filling my mind with all kinds of knowledge in a frenzied attempt to receive answers to my questions. Every paragraph of every book seemed to be written just for me, and I filled the book margins with notes and thoughts. I read everything I could get my hands on, including philosophy, theology, new age, self-help, psychology, poetry, biographies, science, and a variety of the greatest writers in human history.

Sadly, although I read the Bible cover to cover twice, I definitively avoided one area of knowledge in my voracious reading. I had purposely avoided anything related to Catholicism. I had been raised Catholic and felt this to be an outdated, outmoded faith that held no answers for me.

Within my reading, particularly in the new age and enlightenment material, I learned that the term "religion" means to bind up and restrict. During my crisis, I was searching for a liberating, deep spirituality that could free me from my nightmare, not bind me up. The last thing I desired was a dead set of precepts, rules, and rituals. For me, this was what Catholicism represented and I thought I already knew everything it contained and taught. For this reason, I opted to move on and *graduate* from this outmoded folly of my childhood.

I would not know that this belief and decision to abandon Catholicism would cause me additional pain as I spent precious months and years seeking answers elsewhere. I now realize that for any faith to ultimately become real for us, it must transcend the mere intellectual plane and involve a real-life experience. Spiritual maturity and religion are two completely different concepts. The internalization of faith was the process occurring for me during this time.

As I continued to read, I began to feel a compulsive need to serve others and volunteer my time to those less fortunate, particularly the elderly and the poor. I cannot explain where this drive emanated from; I just knew I HAD to do it. Surprisingly, I began to feel my hurt and pain diminish as I gave myself away in local nursing homes, a homeless shelter, a community thrift store, a local service organization and as I coached Madison's sports teams and volunteered at her school events.

The more I gave, the less pain I felt. Occasionally, I even went a couple of days without dwelling on my ordeal at all! Looking back, I see how these many hours of service became like deeply rooted seeds within me because of the intense nature of my pain. As a result, an unshakable drive to lift up the poor, vulnerable, and marginalized of society developed, and I am certain it will remain with me for the remainder of my life.

It was during these months that I also began to visit churches. I was seeking a faith community that would provide support and answers to my suffering. In those days, I was a completely open vessel and searched everywhere. I would jump at the first opportunity for membership upon discovering a new Christian church or faith.

My search took me from one end of the Christian landscape to the other and then beyond. I recall being in a Houston, Texas, hotel lobby during this period and noticing a copy of *Science and Health*, the Christian Scientist bible, on the hotel bookshelf. Its seemingly perfect synthesis between religion and health resonated with me as a doctor, and I felt God had placed that book there just for me.

When I returned home, I purchased a copy, read it cover to cover, and visited a Christian Scientist church. After attending two or three scientist churches, I discovered that the teachings possessed significant contradiction and faulty logic that became immediately apparent. Despite being aggressively recruited, I decided this was not for me and moved on.

For some time, I also dove headlong into the new age movement and began attending the Unity Church and the various related Science of Mind churches. I embraced their positive message entirely and attempted to immediately put it to work in my life. Their positive message of love was comforting to me and validated the beliefs I held at the time. The message denounced the harms and evils of organized religion, especially Catholicism.

The new age movement and its churches for the first time exposed me to teachings about the nonexistence of Hell, Satan, evil, sin, and objective moral law (or definitive right and wrong). The new age movement taught me that these are just man-made constructs created within our own minds. I was taught how these doctrines had developed as a result of the oppressive teachings of organized religion through the centuries, for the purpose of instilling guilt and maintaining authority and power over the faithful.

Much effort is needed, according to this philosophy, to rid ourselves of this *mental conditioning* and to begin to change our thinking by positive affirmation and meditation. I learned that if a person finds himself or herself suffering at the moment, the suffering is entirely a product of the individual's thinking. Conversely, the same suffering could be affirmed away by a change in this very thinking. I absolutely loved and accepted these teachings and wanted desperately for them to work!

It was around this time that Laura and I were served with a $40,000 lawsuit brought against me by a creditor of the Russians, who had long since skipped town. Laura and I were the only people the creditor could find. As seemingly ridiculous as it sounds, we were forced to go into considerable debt and hire a civil attorney to represent us and eventually go to trial to fight this. I saw the new age movement much differently after this event.

I quickly discovered that the positive new age message works fine, as long as life goes smoothly. During this civil suit, however, I discovered that when life becomes difficult and you reach out for this soft foundation of superficiality, you immediately sink like a rock. You desperately attempt to cling to the positive principles that were taught, but your grasp finds only thin air.

Sadly, I witnessed this experience over and over again. The vast majority of Unity Church attendees and other metaphysical new age/new-thought devotees I met were pure, gentle souls experiencing great amounts of pain and suffering within their lives. Many of them possessed great guilt because they were convinced that it was only their thinking bringing about their suffering, and they had no idea what their next steps should be.

Although disguised within the indisputable Christian ideals of love, acceptance, and peace, the new age movement entices these desperate souls to cling to its positive message, a message possessing a thin overlying veneer of comfort but that ultimately retreats at the first sign of life's struggles. I and others in pain were enamored and enthralled by these enchanted teachings of heaven. Unfortunately, we were never taught the way to get there.

The final place I found myself during this period in the wilderness was a very bizarre group called Search for God. Search for God is an organization based in Virginia Beach, Virginia, that is devoted to the writings of a self-proclaimed psychic and healer named Edgar Cayce who lived in the early twentieth century. Cayce's voluminous works offer extensive healings, as well as explanations of the Bible based on his knowledge of the reincarnated identities of each Bible character, including Christ. Although several of Cayce's healings have been medically documented, he nonetheless includes himself on this list as a primary reincarnated Bible character.

The Search for God groups are organized throughout the world and meet weekly in members' living rooms for two hours of psychic readings, prayer, and new age meditation and discussion. I spent many enjoyable months within one of these groups, until one day Laura gently but worriedly made a suggestion that would change our lives.

* * *

Over these many months of searching, significant strain and tension had been placed upon our marriage. It was as if I had fallen overboard into the ocean, desperately thrashing around and trying to cling to a life raft. In my thrashing, I had been forced to take my eye off other priorities, namely Laura. A distance had begun to develop between us as we moved in opposite directions.

I had set off on a self-absorbed search for answers and purpose, looking for my life raft. Laura, however, had made a loving choice that was very difficult for her, particularly as a mother. She had decided to let me go, allowing distance, in hopes that I would eventually find what I was looking for and return home. In hindsight, although difficult, this decision was a marriage saver.

Increasingly, however, Laura was experiencing a growing sense of unavoidable anger when she thought of the future reality of her family and the end of us as we knew it. In Laura's eyes, she had purposely married a good man who was also a good father, and this man was soon going to be taken out of the picture. She could not shake the question in her head as she thought about what was happening to us: Why was God allowing her family to be ripped apart and allowing Madison to lose a good father? As we both struggled upon our divergent paths, our distance manifested each evening as I spent the night engrossed in piles of books, while she shared her bed with Madison.

It was within this context of increasingly divergent paths and my newfound devotion to the psychic healing group that Laura decided to step in and bring rationality back to my search. May all of us be blessed with such a loving influence of moderation in our lives when we wander too far to the extremes. After many months of patience, Laura became convinced I was turning into a misguided religious nut and had lost my way. Despite her Protestant Evangelical background, she made her suggestion. "Mike, why don't you go see a priest."

Play Offense with Life

The potential of our lives can be summed up very quickly each morning of every new day. Despite our age, upon awaking each morning, how do we view life? Do we see it as a beginning or an ending? If we see every morning as a new beginning with lives to touch and a difference to make in our families and our world, we are living blessed lives. If not, God has a plan for us to show us that our best days are not behind us.

To be certain, life is not fair in this world. Many of us are hit by unfortunate circumstances that will be fully understood only in the next life. But will this be the last chapter of our book or the first chapter? Our power of choice holds the answer to this question as well as to several others.

Problems and change will always occur as two of life's enduring constants. Do not resist them. They are frequently God's way of making progress. It remains up to us, however, and our power of choice, to decide where these two constants shall lead us. Are the inevitable problems and changes of life leading to continued growth and expansion or merely serving as an endless succession of painful experience, overwhelming obstacles, and an aimless wandering through a vast wilderness?

God's nature is one of creation and expansion. He knows no other. We can choose to accept and conform to this or to steadfastly resist it. Every one of God's new doorways presented to us is bigger than the previous ones. We must have the courage to choose them, leave the past behind and then walk through these new doorways.

Surrender the myth of being in control. If we are doing our best, the future is in God's hands. If He holds our future, it is brighter than we could ever imagine.

Do you wish to see the future? Ask Him to show you a glimpse. God already resides in our future and will show us His dreams for our lives. His glimpse of our future is usually the apex of what He knows we are capable of. It simply remains up to us to get to work building the foundations and filling in the gaps. Put yourself daily in His glimpse of your future and bring it increasingly into reality. When one person does this, all of us win.

Pray unceasingly. (1 Thess 5:17) After God shows you your future, proceed with reckless abandon. Embrace His dreams with courage and reject timidity, caution, and fear. Take bold action and think bold thoughts, and you will begin to feel great. Each morning presents a new opportunity to "fail" forward fast into God's bigger dreams for us.

In the sporting world, goals are not scored on defense. Similarly, life is best played on offense. Proactively choose the problems and changes that will make us, instead of passively reacting to those that could break us. Begin to see change, no matter how difficult, as a beginning rather than an ending. The potential of our lives is built upon the choices we make amid these most difficult times.

Awaken tomorrow morning as if God's dreams depend upon it. Will we choose to act or be acted upon? There will be plenty of time soon enough to catch up on rest and look back on our life's work alongside Him in His kingdom.

CHAPTER FIVE:

A New Creation

"Wisdom is worthless without grace. But when wisdom is joined with grace and its work becomes perfect... this is called regeneration. And with a tranquil conscience and an assured innocence, this leads to a blessed life."

Unknown

I HAD SPENT NEARLY TWO years traversing the Christian landscape in the form of books, churches, groups, and organizations, and now I found myself right back where I had determined not to go, Catholicism. After a meager resistance to Laura's suggestion, I called and made an appointment with a new parish priest who had just been assigned to our local parish. With very little hope of any answers, I went to meet with him as I had promised Laura.

Although I had grown up Catholic, I had never before met with a priest and spoken with one alone face to face. As a child, I had respected the priesthood but also kept a healthy distance, carrying a fear of relating to them as normal people. I had no idea where this fear came from, but it followed me into adulthood right up to this particular day.

As I entered Father John's office, something immediately felt different. A pervasive peacefulness seemed to draw me in. I was struck by the hundreds of books upon his office bookshelves. Along with the books were a wide assortment of statues of various saints. His walls were adorned by a large crucifix and a portrait of Mary, the mother of Jesus. I couldn't help but think about how, just a few moments ago, I had wanted no part of all the dead precepts, rules, and rituals contained within these books and relics. Now, however, this nonthreatening feeling of peace within Father John's office had me intrigued.

"Hello, Michael. It's nice to meet you. Have a seat so we can talk for a while. Let's go ahead and start with a prayer."

Father John was a kind, gentle, ordinary man like many I had met before. He laughed often, and when he wasn't laughing, the spark in his eyes made him appear as if he was. When he spoke with me, it felt as if I was the most important person in the world to him, and it was exciting to be around the light of his soul.

What made Father John particularly special, however, was the deep, unwavering convictions he held and his love for God. I instantly perceived him to be a man of great courage and someone who would die for these convictions. In the months and years of my searching, I had come across many claims of those who had found truth. In that instant, I realized that real truth is something you are willing to bet your life on. Unlike the others, in Father John, I had met someone who would actually give his life for truth and die with a smile upon his face. I wanted this for myself.

I began to meet with Father John every other week and could not wait for my next one-hour session. My eyes were being opened to a *new* Catholic Church. It was within this exciting discovery that I found the answers to my questions in a place I had never thought I would. But first, a Catholic demolition and reconstruction project was needed.

As a cradle Catholic, one born into Catholicism, I'd had the misfortune of falling within the lost generation. These were the years following the mid-1960s Vatican II period until the late 1980s. During this time, a push had been made to soften church teachings in an attempt to mediate the strict pre-1960s Catholic approach. Although in theory this made sense, the unfortunate effect had been the creation of millions of Catholics who had not learned their faith and, like me, had fallen into the lukewarm waters of surface Catholicism.

As I met with Father John for biweekly spiritual direction, he methodically began to take me through Catholic teaching. Upon hearing my story, he started with the beautiful Catholic theology of suffering. In my years of searching, no one had remotely pretended to offer a satisfactory explanation to the question of human suffering, including my extensive non-Catholic book list. Father John explained thoroughly and clarified the questions that had been confounding me.

I learned that we shall all be given a cross to carry in this life and we need not run from it or spend our lives attempting to avoid it. Just as Christ had, by carrying our crosses, whatever they may be, with courage, strength, and dignity, we begin to receive and usher forth grace into our world. These graces, through this redemptive process, go forth and lift up others who are experiencing suffering and trials but may be too weak to lift themselves. By carrying our sufferings in this way, we may be saving our children and our children's children from untold trials, sufferings, and difficult life choices of their own!

I learned that through the carrying of one's cross and the ensuing transmission of grace, it is possible that a heroin addict on the other side of the world will suddenly find the strength to put down the needle and seek help. Similarly, a young woman across town tonight may suddenly find the courage to turn around from the abortion clinic and seek other options.

"The only question that remains, Michael, is whether we will choose to be strong enough to courageously carry our burdens for the purpose of transmitting our grace to others," Father John explained.

Father John explained how this occurs by teaching me about the beauty of the Mystical Body of Christ. This redemptive principle can occur because we are all part of an interconnected web of souls, currently living and deceased, with Christ as our head. I learned that it is okay to live with some mystery presently, but we should eagerly await (instead of fear) the General Judgment, when we shall all be gathered together at the end of time. This is when all of our actions, heroic or small, will finally be revealed and all can see how they impacted the Mystical Body as a whole! I left some of our meetings with my head spinning for hours as the implication of these realities slowly sank in.

Father John and I made a great team. As I excitedly listened and took in everything he said, his tremendous zeal for ministry became even more ignited. Not quite a decade out of seminary, Father John was not immune to periodic discouragement and disappointment with apathetic parishioners. He put everything he had into his inspiring, fiery sermons and one-on-one counseling sessions. Inevitably, when some in a congregation fail to hear the message and transform their lives, it is painful. It can leave a pastor physically depleted, depressed, and burned-out. In me, Father John had an open instrument for God's grace. I was increasingly gaining a belief and faith that I would die for. This is inspiring for any pastor.

The next teaching Father John went into was reconciliation, or confession. Christ knew fully well that every human being needed to hear three short words: *You are forgiven.* As Catholics, when we confess, we not only confess our sins to God but also must confess to our brothers and sisters within the Mystical Body whom we have greatly harmed. In the past, I had failed to see the need for this beautiful sacrament, opting instead to keep it between me and God. I now realized that from the very beginning, Christ has always used human beings to carry out His will and purpose for our lives. In other words, if we truly are God's covenant family, we must start acting like one.

When Father John asked me if I was ready to make a confession, I initially hesitated, hoping he would forget. There could be no way I could bring myself to share my decades of sin with another human being! After all, my last confession had been my first and only one, when I was seven years old. After all these decades, I still recalled confessing those sins, which mainly involved hitting my seven-year-old next-door-neighbor best friend with a stick.

Father John persisted, however, so the date was set, and I began to prepare an examination of my life over the past two decades. Painfully, this included a rebellious and embarrassing high school and college period that I would rather have forgotten. I briefly thought about canceling our next appointment and telling Father John I was too busy, but only briefly. The inspiration of his courage and his deep convictions were too strong, and I greatly desired to possess them for myself. For this reason, I came back prepared for our next visit and made my first confession since elementary school.

As I began, my voice was shaky with a mixture of nervousness, fear, and embarrassment. It felt as if I were naked before God. Much like the story of the prodigal son who returned to his father, I was ashamed for disappointing Him and was willing to accept whatever punishment He deemed fit for my wayward life. As I staggered my way through the mud of my high school and college experiences, recounting those whom I had hurt, I carefully watched Father John's facial expressions for disappointment, surprise, or outright shock.

To my relief, Father John sat calmly with his kind, friendly, and peaceful expression never wavering. Instead of becoming uncomfortably shocked and having his ears turn red like I expected, Father John gave *me* a most unexpected shock. He imitated a loving father acting toward his child. In the story, as the prodigal son came within sight of his home, his father ran out to meet him halfway. This was my experience with God's love. After decades of holding on to these burdens, which I had fooled myself into thinking I was ignoring, Father John instantly took them from me in complete non-judgment. I had felt like I was the only one dragging these heavy burdens around and was resigned to keep them to myself. I discovered instead that my sins were nothing new and I was no different than the rest of a fallen humanity. Carrying these burdens throughout our lives is not what God desires of us.

"Michael, I absolve you of all your sins in the name of the Father, the Son, and the Holy Spirit," Father John said with a friendly smile.

For the first time in my life, I actually *felt* grace as it rushed in and flooded my soul. The years of regret fell away like sandbags. I walked out of his office that day as if on a cloud, with twenty-plus years of weight immediately off my soul. Outside, the sun was shining more brightly in my eyes. I could also take the deepest and most unrestricted breath of fresh air into my lungs that I'd had in many years. What a feeling of renewal and healing I experienced! Confession is a sacrament of healing, and I found it to be health for my mind, body, and soul.

The next teaching Father John went into was the Holy Eucharist, Christ's body and blood. In my years of surface Catholicism, I had never been taught the doctrine of the Real Presence. I learned that I was actually receiving the <u>real</u> body and blood of Christ in a re-presentation of His sacrifice in which I can become a part of. My walk up to Holy Communion after this took on a newfound eternal realization for me.

I learned that the words of consecration spoken by the priest open up the doorway between heaven and earth. All constraints of space and time are broken down and the Mystical Body's communion of souls, living and deceased, are unified. Nowhere in life will we ever experience the reality of Heaven more closely than at Mass with the Eucharist. This understanding provided a spiritual balance to my life at a time when my life was careening out of control. It allowed me one foot in eternity while the other remained firmly planted within this world.

I began attending daily Mass and receiving our Lord in this beautiful sacrament. The King of the universe was now present to me as a former surface Catholic, and I was determined to spend my time making up for the years I had lost. During particular periods of difficulty, I remember the consolation of counting down the hours until the next day's daily Mass and the opportunity to receive our Lord again.

As the weeks began to pass, I felt an inner strength developing within me each time I received our Lord in daily Mass. The Eucharist served as a means of growth to my Christian life. Even though I was being ravaged by the incredible stresses of my ordeal, this seemed to be merely an external attack on my outer body. The renewal and inspiration I was gaining by what my inner body was becoming was far greater. (2 Cor 4:16) I began to almost separate myself in this manner, grasping for the real priorities of life: pleasing God and my family, lifting up others who were suffering, and standing up for truth and justice. Daily reception of the Eucharist brought these higher eternal priorities more forcefully to the surface and pushed away the lower priorities of fear, anxiety, and meaningless temporal pursuits.

If I had stopped to look at myself, I probably would not have recognized the person I was becoming. In addition, my inner strength began to rub off on my family as they received the strength to endure this ordeal by God's grace working through me. Our family, after enduring some painful distance, was now coming back together through a foundation that would unite us for eternity.

I began to live each day with eternity implanted firmly at the forefront of my mind. This time in my life was when the birds seemed to sing louder, sunsets seemed to burn brighter, and rainbows seemed to have been placed in the sky just for my family and myself. I was growing so close to God that I could feel His very thoughts, wisdom, and guidance, and I conformed my life to this. Over these months, I was stripped bare and became an emptied earthen vessel. I was completely surrendering as an instrument of His will, and He was filling me up and remolding me into a new creation with His hands.

At this point, Father John taught me several practices and tools so I could sustain this Christian growth. One of those was authentic Christian prayer and meditation. Being freshly plucked out of the new age movement, I was very familiar with meditation. The differences were like night and day, however. The new age meditation I had been exposed to had taught me to *empty* myself to the noise and distractions of the world so as to achieve self-realization. As this emptiness occurred, I could more capably focus on my personal ideals. In other words, new age thought was an emptying process focused on ourselves, further adding to the tragic epidemic of selfishness of our time.

Instead, I learned that the authentic Christian meditation taught by the mystics involved a *filling* process rather than an emptying. During meditation, we are filling ourselves with the love and ideals of

Christ, our perfect teacher and the fulfillment of all earthly wisdom and philosophies. By so doing, we are very often led to lift up others rather than selfishly focus on personal ideals. In other words, the filling process of Christian meditation is *life-giving*, versus the new age *life-draining* process of emptying.

Father John also taught me about the practice of fasting and how to more deeply root my charitable endeavors in Christ. He revamped my reading list by pointing me toward some of the great Christian mystics throughout history. Far from my past perceptions of Catholic literature being mere precepts, rules, and rituals, I found a 2000-year treasury of inspired writings. These writings spoke directly to my situation, and I grew tremendously from the wisdom of St. John of the Cross, St. Therese, St. Theresa of Avila, and others.

I was also encouraged to spend time at a local Carmelite monastery. The Carmelites are a beautiful religious order created around silent prayer, meditation, and growing in intimate union with Christ. I enjoyed my time with the Carmelites extremely. I must say, if I had not already chosen my vocation of married family life, I would have been very tempted to stay within those peacefully tranquil monastic walls. For me, religion was no longer seen as a binding restriction of faith. It had now become a free and deep spirituality that was palpably alive and real within my life.

* * *

This exciting period of renewal for me reached an incredible high point, with an experience that forever changed the lives of Laura and I. Despite this growth, I was still experiencing periodic times of extreme difficulty when my stress, anxiety, and fatigue gained the upper hand and had their way with me. It was on one of these occasions, when I was having a particularly difficult night of sleep, that I decided to get up and pray the rosary rather than ruin another night of Laura's sleep.

At about 2:00 a.m., in the dark, silent stillness of our home, I went into the front bedroom and sat on the edge of the bed. My back was facing the closed door. From there, I had a perfect view of the full moon, brightly shining through the arched windows above. As I sat in the moonlight, I began to pray the rosary. I had hoped to fight off the overwhelming feeling of anxiety that had overtaken me that night.

A short time later, Laura awoke. Realizing I was not in bed, she went searching for me. As she opened the door to the bedroom in which I was praying, I was able to turn around just in time to see her bolting out of the room, quickly shutting the door behind her.

"Laura, it's okay. You can come in."

"Can you just come out here?" she replied timidly, standing just outside the door.

Immediately, I went out to her to see if she was okay. What she told me bordered on the amazing and gave both of us the inspiration and strength to fight on and carry our cross, knowing God's will was being done.

"Mike, your room was full of people. They were all around you. I don't know who they all were, but one was your grandmother and one was Mary!"

Although I had seen nothing, I remembered and felt their loving presence return to me after Laura told me this. Like successfully recapturing a dream that had long ago faded from consciousness, the strong, vivid familiarity left me stunned. No further words were necessary. I knew. I also knew and realized they had been with me on other occasions as well. Through Laura, God had permitted me to notice them. Laura said she had left the room not really out of fear but out of a feeling as if she were disturbing us. She felt she had walked in on something in which she was not invited! I told her how extremely alone, uncertain, and lost I had felt while I had just been praying.

"Mike, you're not alone," she replied.

We were both unaware of what awaited our family in just a few short weeks. It had been almost twenty-eight months since that dreadful May 1 phone call from the government. What had then been a period of helpless fear and despairing hopelessness for me, I now saw much differently. In these twenty-eight months, I felt as if I had traveled a lifetime from who I had been. As my captors silently approached on the morning of August 9, 1999, they would encounter a new creation in me and in my family. We were ready to face the persecution, stand for truth and justice, and do the will of the Father, no matter how difficult it would become.

Our Regenerative Magnificence

Take a moment to contemplate the miracle within each of us. We are given our sight through 100 million receptors within the eyes. We are given our hearing through 25,000 vibratory fibers within the ears. We are given our motion through the coordination of 600 muscles, 200 bones, and 7 miles of nerve fiber. We receive our oxygen through 600 million compartments of folded tissue within the lungs. We are supplied our blood through the miracle of the human heart as it beats 35 million times per year, pumping 600,000 gallons of blood per year through 60,000 miles of veins, arteries, and vessels. Most miraculously, we have been given our human brains. At birth, we have more than 100 billion brain cells and connections, exceeding even the stars in our galaxy. Within the brain's 6 pounds, we possess nearly 1000 trillion nerve synapses filing away every incident and experience since birth and giving us virtually limitless processing capability. The miracle does not stop here, however.

The human body possesses 75 trillion cells, all in communication with each other as the vital processes of life are carried out. Through this communication, without so much as a conscious thought from us, one of these processes replaces dead and dying cells with new, healthy cells. It is happening now, in each of us, particularly when we sleep.

The miracle of the human body becomes more profound as we discover that we are being created anew in each instant. Two million new blood cells are created each second to replace two million dead ones. In all, each hour, the body creates one *billion* new cells! Each of us has new intestines every 2 to 3 days, a new stomach lining every 5 days, new skin every 28 days, a new liver every 42 days, and new bones every 90 days.

This renewal process replaces the old at lightning speeds with an innate wisdom and communication beyond human understanding. A writer once reminded us to think of the body not as a machine but as a river. This regenerative river that we call the human body is what allows us to heal.

The continuous death and resurrection of our bodies has occurred since birth and will continue until death, or when the new, healthy cells cease replicating at pace with the dead and dying ones. This type of perfection and complexity can only point us to a Creator with an even greater perfection and complexity than that which we possess. St. Thomas Aquinas perfectly captured this idea when he described God as a Being in which all pure perfection is found in an infinite degree.

The regenerative nature of the human body and our cell replication follow a process of repetition. This process relies heavily upon our existing "patterned structures" and lifestyle habits as a guide. This is fine as long as we are healthy. If we become ill, however, this becomes a problem.

In other words, a forty-year cigarette smoker with lung cancer cells will not suddenly develop new, healthy lung cells as he or she continues the smoking habit. The new replacement cells will merely follow the patterned structure unless changes are made to the contrary. The human organism, biochemically and neurologically, is one continuous habitual process, moving us toward either health or illness depending on our choices. This process never remains still. The essence of health and healing, therefore, lies in consciously choosing and increasingly creating a new, thriving, and vibrant internal environment, or patterned structure, each and every day. This allows the body to replicate itself with new, healthy cells instead of unhealthy ones and move us toward greater health. This has considerable spiritual implications.

The harm wrought by original sin is "hardwired" into our very neurology and ceaselessly works against us. Like our health, our spiritual lives are never standing still. The negative relationships, bad habits, negative feelings, addictions, and sins of the past and present promote the growth of adverse neurological tracts and neural pathways within our nervous systems. In other words, we get addicted to the adverse, as we need more and more of the sin (alcohol, sex, greed, hate, food, drugs, etc.) to satiate our desires.

The regenerative grace of God is available to us at every moment of life. If we choose to accept this grace, we can instantly begin to change, in a way that allows the grace and wisdom of God to regenerate and recreate our bodies in His image. Grace builds upon nature. We must do our part, however, by changing lifestyle habits that obstruct God's grace, replacing them with new choices, creating a new, thriving, and vibrant spiritual environment for grace to build upon. Just like healing, this process takes time.

Our time is brief. Start today. We need to fast, pray, and receive Christ's gift of the Holy Eucharist often. As we do, we become infused with new life. We are becoming what we are receiving. We can now radiate what we have become. The trillions of cells within us begin to vibrate at a supernatural level as they are renewed with light, essentially flooding our neurology. Bathe your cells in this light of God's regenerative grace always!

CHAPTER SIX:

O Death, Where Is Thy Sting?

"Fear is only six inches deep."

Unknown

MONDAY, AUGUST 9, 1999, WAS a scorching hot Texas summer day. It was also a very special day for our family. At 7:00 p.m. that evening, Laura and I would be attending Madison's kindergarten orientation meeting in preparation for her first day of school two days later. We would meet the teachers and administration and hear of the curriculum and field trips for the upcoming school year.

Just five years old, Madison always seemed to be ahead of her years. From a young age, she had a strong, quiet confidence and a compassionate heart immediately noticed by all those around her. Laura and I have always been proud of this fact. Although Madison has always possessed a beauty and unique poise about her, Laura and I know that the real attraction to Madison is a light-filled grace that she unwittingly radiates to those around her.

This was an exciting time as our daughter was growing up and starting a new school. We felt that a new phase of our lives was beginning, and we were determined not to miss a second of it. And, in the back of my mind, I knew there were no guarantees I would witness another first day of school at any time in the near future.

On another front, Laura was starting her first day of work in the corporate office of a large office-furniture distributor in our area. She had returned to work to support our family through this ordeal. Laura left early that morning of August 9, and I was going to take Madison to Laura's mother before I went to work at my practice.

Madison was on the couch watching cartoons as I was ironing my shirt in the hallway. We were talking about how great her first day of kindergarten was going to be.

"Madie, you are going to love it. There is nothing to be nervous about," I reassured her as she smiled back.

Just then, I heard the doorbell ring, followed by a loud knock on the door. Playdoh started barking, and I went to the front door to look through the peep hole. I saw several men in navy-blue jackets with the distinctive yellow FBI insignia. I was not the least bit surprised as I opened the door. I was face-to-face with six FBI agents in flak jackets, assault weapons drawn.

"We're here for Michael Norman in response to a criminal indictment. Is that you?"

After saying yes, I was rushed by the agents and forced face-first into the wall as my hands were handcuffed behind my back. They read me my rights and asked if anybody else was in the house.

"Just my daughter," I answered with my face still pressed into the wall and an agent's forearm compressing my neck.

Not waiting for my answer, they filed in and begin combing through the house. After searching the house, three of the agents left, leaving me in the custody of the remaining three agents. Of these, one was the lead agent of this raid and a face that was familiar to me.

FBI Lead Agent Stone was one of the henchmen U.S. Attorney Hill had dispatched to the elevator that day after my court testimony. Now it was apparent he was on another mission. Hill had obviously instructed him to send a strong message.

Agent Stone was another character in our ordeal who left a unique impression on both Laura and me. He was moderately short in stature, with a painstakingly perfect head of dark coifed hair and a distinct swagger that hinted of insecurity; it was very apparent that his position was important to him. Agent Stone reminded me of the kid on the elementary school playground who was always the last one picked for all the sports teams. He struck me as one who had maneuvered his way into a position of power and now exacted revenge for all the perceived slights of his childhood. For Laura, however, her later opinion of him would be much more clear-cut. After just one glance at the vainglorious image of Agent Stone, who enkindled memories of the arrogant courtroom figures of her painful childhood, Laura's fighting instincts would shift into high gear.

Agent Stone was the first agent through my door that morning and made sure to use a little extra force in pushing me into the wall and handcuffing me. This was to clearly show me who was boss and in full control of the situation. He seemed to enjoy every minute of it despite his ability to keep a serious look on his face throughout.

Initially, Agent Stone threatened to place Madison into the custody of Social Services for the day. Thankfully, I was successful in explaining that my mother-in-law, Dee, was only twenty minutes away and could be there quickly. I called Dee, waking her up with my startling news, and asked her to rush over to my house. The next call I made was to one of my office staff to cancel all my patients for that day.

With nothing more to do but wait, I went into my living room and sat with Madison on the couch to watch an episode of *Rugrats*. As I very calmly reassured and hugged her while laughing at the cartoon, I sat next to the strongest rock I had ever seen. She stayed extremely calm and relaxed with me as she endured what a five-year-old should never have to endure.

When Dee arrived, Stone and another agent stood behind me as I sat on the couch while another younger FBI agent sat at my dining room table, reading my morning newspaper. Just as in Laura, a fiery instinct to fight became aroused in my mother-in-law. She had valiantly risen above the challenges and struggles of her early years by working two jobs and raising her two girls by herself. Her life had been difficult, but she had succeeded through hard work and courage. Now, with the turmoil of her early life many years removed, I sensed a return of her anger toward the cruel injustice being inflicted upon her family resurfacing once again.

With glaring eye contact upon the agents, Dee walked straight by them to Madison and picked her granddaughter up into her arms, remarking, "Go find real criminals! This is just guilt by association."

"Hey, it's gonna be all right. Now we can get it over with. It's the waiting that was the hardest," I told her calmly and reassuringly.

She returned no comment, only a long stare that possessed both respect and fear. By this time, the young FBI agent had gotten up from my newspaper and was listening in on my reassuring words to Dee. Apart from the other two agents, I could sense this one particular agent was really focused in on our interaction. Although it would never be admitted, I felt a deep, unspoken admiration from him as he watched us.

"I love you, Madie," I said as I kissed my daughter good-bye.

The agents allowed Dee to take Madison down the hall so she would not see her father re-handcuffed. I was then led outside to an awaiting dark four-door Town Car parked in front of my home.

I was placed in the backseat with the young FBI agent who had witnessed the scene between Dee, Madison, and myself. As we drove off, the young agent next to me remarked how calm and strong my daughter was and the fact that his daughter would have been hysterical. Having confirmed my suspicions of his admiration for our household's strength, I replied very cordially.

"Yeah. She's as strong as a rock." I thought of how I was already missing her.

After that day, it would be several years before Madison could hear our doorbell ring at home and not run, terrified, into another room to hide. Nonetheless, I could not have been any prouder of Madison and my entire family in that moment.

As Agent Stone drove me away, he asked me for an alternate route to the Dallas Tollway after receiving a bad traffic report on the radio. I graciously gave him directions like I was talking to my best friend in the front seat. I wondered if they were questioning why U.S. Attorney Hill had ordered them to conduct a fully armed, early morning six-man raid on the home of such a seemingly nice family. At least I was hoping they would question this. It was just after thinking this thought that I decided to pull away from this nightmare and surrender to the peace and serenity that can be found only in our Lord.

I began to silently recite the twenty-third Psalm, over and over. Peace overtook my body, and I felt absolutely invincible to the arrows of this world. I was tightly handcuffed in the backseat of that car as it cruised south down the Dallas Tollway toward federal prison. If I had been headed toward my actual crucifixion that morning, I could not have been more prepared and ready. I was confident that I was doing God's will and that I was not alone.

I was led upstairs into the FBI offices by Agent Stone, who proudly paraded his catch past fifteen to twenty of his fellow agents who were just standing around watching. They took every opportunity to project an air of intimidation toward me. I was then photographed and fingerprinted by the proud lead agent who had successfully led the raid at my home.

The entire time, I remained absolutely respectful, calm and silent, as it seemed I was being watched by the entire office of male and female agents. It almost felt as if I was some famous trophy criminal that everybody had been expecting that morning. As I found myself hopelessly within the grip of ultimate human power, I stuck out like a sore thumb, I should like to think, compared to their usual high-level criminals, murderers, drug dealers, and rapists.

After this, I was led back down to the parking garage, from where I would be taken to the federal detention center fifteen minutes away. As I was being put in the backseat of the car, I discovered whom my backseat passenger would be. With his part of the dirty work complete, he would now surface from behind the shadows and get into the car with me as I was taken to prison. In an arrogant and smug manner, Agent Stone took no time in introducing us.

"Dr. Norman, you remember Agent Hennessey of the Secret Service, don't you?"

"You mean the IRS," I calmly replied.

Both men started laughing.

"Well, he's got a good memory," Hennessey remarked sarcastically, which only seemed to draw more of their laughter.

I instantly recognized the twisted facial expression and sinister smirk of the man who had procured the false confession from me almost two and a half years before. Equally recognizable was the familiar apologetic tone of voice that had been ingrained within me since that May 1 phone call to my home threatening my family. Somehow, he managed to keep all these oddities intact, just as I had remembered them from our first encounter at the Secret Service office interview so long ago.

"Well, Dr. Norman. What are you going to do?" He was still playing his friendly good-cop role.

"I'm going to straighten everything out," I replied.

"Did they explain why they indicted you?" he continued with his unceasing smirk intact.

"No," I said.

"Well, it was because of all your admissions in our interview. You admitted to us that you were part of all this," he said, his smile broadening as he waited to see my reaction.

I turned away, looking out my window and remaining perfectly silent for the remainder of the trip. I looked out at the people of downtown Dallas, on the sidewalks and in their cars and proceeding along with their ordinary Monday. I am certain everybody I saw that day had a long and unlimited list of their own worries, concerns, and problems. Just the same, however, I remember thinking, *You would not believe what is happening to me right now*!

* * *

Increasingly, in our day and age, it seems that there is a very thin distinction between good and evil. In August 1999, this line became patently obvious to me. My life—family, friends, and even my existence—was just an expendable pawn within this game that had been conjured up against me by these lesser forms of humanity. The feeling was also very eerie. In a matter of two short hours, I had been suddenly plucked from my previous existence and forcibly pulled down into their world. It was a pit of deceit, immorality, greed, power, dishonesty, detached emotional immaturity, and superficiality and was void of any type of compassion or humanness. A world of atheistic humanism exists side by side with our world, and I had never before encountered it. This world was darker than anything I had experienced with the Russian Mafia.

Now that I was face to face with this world of human power, I had never been so much at peace and full of love. I fully knew that I was firmly entrenched on the side of good with truth and justice as my companions, in opposition to this world of human power complete with its repulsive emptiness. I was certainly aware that I was about to be painfully crushed under the tentacles of the government's power. Nonetheless, I could not help but smiling to myself as I looked out the window at the beautiful world of humanity that I had just been plucked from. At that moment, I completely surrendered and was ready for the persecution to come.

We arrived at the federal detention center in a secure underground parking area, and the three of us got into a nondescript steel elevator absent of carpet, floor numbers, or even buttons. It was obviously an elevator that went to only one place.

The two agents released me into the custody of a young Hispanic male in his upper twenties and then promptly disappeared. This prison guard, in complete businesslike fashion, began the normal routine of admitting a new inmate as he had done countless times before, judging from his cool manner. I silently attempted to connect and relate to him through such subtleties as eye contact, demeanor, and facial gestures, but I quickly sensed that to him, I was just another scumbag criminal. I was now firmly in his world.

It was immediately obvious that this seemingly ordinary individual was extremely proud of his position of respect and power within these prison walls. What a strange realization that I came to at this instant: the feeling of being a second-class citizen and nothing more than a caged animal. In that instant, my love and empathy for the less fortunate of society, which had been steadily building throughout this ordeal, took another giant leap. Like with Laura, the conviction of fighting for the underdog against the powerful of our world was now firmly implanted within me.

The prison guard took me to a room that looked like a high school nurse's office. He began taking down more personal information on his admitting forms. I then had to empty my pockets as he carefully inventoried and stored everything I had. I dreaded what I knew would come next. Upon his command, I had to strip down and throw my articles of clothing into a distant corner of the room, one at a time while he inspected them. After that, totally naked, I had to turn to face the wall and wait for his commands. After the guard was convinced I had no weapons, he told me to get dressed while he watched and then led me to my cell.

I was led to the cell right around the corner and noticed it was already occupied by a prisoner. He was a large, heavyset Hispanic man in his early thirties. I looked down at the floor as I entered and sat down on the stainless steel bench opposite this man. At first I continued to look down and spoke only when spoken to. It helped the tension that I could also view from our cell an exterior window that was across the corridor I had just walked down. I looked out from the caged windows and enjoyed the view, being able to see for a great distance because of our upper-floor location high above downtown Dallas. I distinctly remember watching the view of the freeway that passed by, which I recognized as Interstate 35, my eventual route home. I stared out at the highway and saw all the cars traveling to their destinations totally unaware of the world that I currently found myself in. They were two separate worlds, divided by iron bars and caged windows, and I wanted desperately to return to the world I had just been taken from.

We were soon joined by three other prisoners who were led, one by one, over a thirty-minute period, into the cell, making a total of five of us. I begin to converse gradually with small talk to the other prisoners, not volunteering much detail. Surprisingly, I began to enjoy this insight and perspective into a world I had never known; however, we were all very wary of the video camera across the corridor, placed above the windows and directed on us the entire time.

The heavyset Hispanic prisoner looked menacing and was known by name to the prison guard, indicating that he was not an average first-time offender. He had his legal papers with him and referred constantly to them, wanting us to become convinced of how flawed and mistaken they were. He claimed he was being tried on double jeopardy, and he wanted each of our legal opinions and interpretations of his papers. The man had actually been brought in by the feds on suspicion of being the Mexican Railway Killer, who was wanted throughout the southwestern U.S. and Mexico at that time. Luckily for me, it turned out that the real killer was caught several months later. At that time, however, it appeared convincing to me that the feds had the right man!

Sitting just to the heavyset Hispanic man's left was a Caucasian man in his late thirties, about six feet tall, with a stocky build and light-brown hair. He was a B.S. artist, for lack of a better term. I recognized this right away, having known many like him back in the real world. I knew this even before his first words to me after he had entered the cell.

"What are you in for, credit cards?" he asked me.

"Nah," I replied.

Then without hesitation he said, "You aren't one of those chiropractors I saw on TV involved in that scam, are you?"

"No, that wasn't me," I said, knowing full well the camera was rolling the whole time.

I had always heard about "jailhouse snitches" before but had always thought they would be better actors than this guy. After this episode, he got the message, because he backed off me and began to converse with all of us equally. He had been picked up by the feds on firearms and weapons charges. I learned that he was already serving a state sentence for murder, and they had just transferred him over from the state facility that day. Regarding the transfer, this guy could not have been happier. He told us about the undesirable conditions in the state system and how this was his ticket to a better home. But the main thing he kept ranting about was how well we were going to get fed now that we were in federal custody. I'll always remember his profane reassurance to us regarding mealtime.

"We gonna eat good today! The fed'll feed ya ass good. State feeds ya like s***; they don't give a damn 'bout the food!"

I agreed and acted excited, but I kept thinking, *I can't believe this has now become a highlight in life for me.*

One fascinating component of the prisoners' personalities I learned about is their ability to quickly size up human nature. Most undoubtedly due to a necessary survival instinct, they learn to probe and read the people around them in a fast, remarkable manner. During the course of our conversations, the convicted murderer found out that I had written a book. Not missing a beat, he told me he was going to order it through the prison's educational system. Although I

will never know for sure, I got the feeling that he thought he was sharing the cell with some celebrity. At the very least, I represented a part
of the world that he had been separated from for a long time or had
quite possibly never before experienced.

Probably not used to such a big captive audience, the Caucasian
put his nonstop B.S. skills into high gear. He proceeded to give all of
us legal advice for our individual situations, which mainly consisted
of pleading guilty for lesser sentences and doing the least amount of
time possible. He told us of his past experiences and betrayals by
court-appointed lawyers and how inept they were. He spoke about
the one lawyer he had hired to fight charges that he stated he had not
committed. After giving the lawyer $10,000 cash, he said, he had
been quickly forced into a plea bargain against his wishes and sent off
to prison.

Strangely, this attorney he was referring to was one of the attorneys Laura had called on that frantic May 1 date when this ordeal
first began. How glad I was not to have hired that lawyer. He
sounded more criminal than the convicts he represented. All in all,
although I would never trust this B.S. artist with anything, I kind of
enjoyed our entertaining jailhouse conversations that day.

The next prisoner, sitting to the right of me, was an African-
American man in his late twenties. He was thin, dressed in an athletic
suit, and like the B.S. artist, never stopped talking the entire day. He
was mainly complaining about the entire legal system in general and
the prejudice and unfairness of it. Although every other word out of
his mouth was a curse word, I actually enjoyed the insight into his
world as well and found him very entertaining.

His crimes were drug related (dealing, possession, etc.), and he
had been picked up by the feds after multiple priors. This time he
apparently had stepped up from the small time and violated some
more serious federal statutes. His main argument was not that he was
innocent—he freely admitted that he had done his crime; rather, his
argument was that the higher-ups in the drug organizations never pay
the price or get prosecuted by the government. Instead, he said, the
little man is targeted because it is easier. I have to admit, from what
I had experienced to that point, I was in total agreement with him. I'll
never forget his profanity-laced tirade to me that summed it all up:
"They got me in here cause some small-time B.S., while the bidness
man is off buyin' 'nother f***in' boat! These f***ers are a joke.
F*** 'em!"

I have to admit he got no argument from us. He was preaching to the choir.

The fourth and final man was the quietest of all, as he just sat back silently and listened to all the conversations. He was a stocky, heavyset Russian man in his early fifties. I learned that he was included within my indictment and had also been picked up that morning. He was very calm and quiet and spoke only when spoken to.

"Did they all come to your house this morning like me?" I asked, speaking up first.

"Yes, very early while we were still in bed," he replied in a thick Russian accent.

Apparently, they had come to his house a couple of hours before they had come to mine. He told me how his wife had been extremely upset by being awakened by the FBI. I didn't really discuss any details of our case with him because it became apparent we had an interested audience beginning to watch and listen in. All other conversations ceased as the other prisoners now looked on, trying to listen, as if we were big-time mobsters discussing our strategy. I could only imagine what they were thinking in their never-ending attempts to size people up as my apparent "connections" translated into newfound respect by the other prisoners. They had no idea I was totally alone, had never met this Russian before, and was actually extremely jealous of him because he was visited by his attorney and I had no legal representation at all.

As the day progressed and the minutes became hours, I had actually begun to feel a strange comradeship with my new friends against the government. Soon, the long-awaited moment that the B.S. artist had been telling us about arrived: *lunchtime!* We each received a decent-sized hamburger that actually tasted very good, despite the grease.

After lunch, I spent the next few hours talking with my new acquaintances, looking out the window, and contemplating just what I was planning to do. Occasionally, it would briefly sink into my consciousness that I had no lawyer, I had no money, I was up against the full fury of the most powerful government in the free world, and I probably would not see my beautiful daughter again as a free man until she was thirteen years old. Thankfully, that brief, dreadful thought would always fade away and I would somehow rejoin the world of productivity, hope, love, and justice after a short absence.

A couple of hours after lunch, after the day had seemingly spilled into a week, the prison guard came to our cell and announced it was time to go to court. I was rejoined by FBI Agent Stone and IRS Agent Hennessey, as they re-handcuffed me and accompanied me into the elevator down to the courtroom for my arraignment. As our elevator doors opened and we stepped out, I soon remembered exactly who I was.

As I was being led into the courtroom, they were just outside the door. The brief look upon the faces of Laura and my mother looked as if they were going to destroy the arrogant agents who were holding me. That brief look will forever stay in my mind. It caused a surge of strength to course through my entire body. I felt as though I could have broken out of the handcuffs that were clamped tightly around my wrists.

"You be strong!" they exhorted me as I was led past them.

It is no small fact that during the final hours upon His cross, Jesus found himself surrounded by strong, faithful women. Looking down from the cross, He was strengthened and fortified primarily by the faces of Mary, His mother, Mary Magdalene, and others after His male disciples were scattered. I have learned the wisdom of always surrounding ourselves with strong, faithful women. In times of trial and crisis, they hold no fear of the male-dominated halls of human power. Strong, faithful women unequivocally say yes to God and are sure to remain loyally by our sides.

Now it was only fitting that I would finally be introduced to the man who was almost singlehandedly behind this entire ordeal. All others so far in this drama had been mere puppets, but he was the puppet master. He held all the strings.

Upon my escorted, handcuffed entrance into his courtroom, U.S. Attorney Hill looked up at me from across the room. He quickly assumed an amused look upon his face at the spectacle of my current predicament. Like a peacock flaunting his feathers, he paraded right up to me.

U.S. Attorney Hill was a large, heavyset man, about sixty years of age, with glasses as thick as coke bottles. He carried himself in such a way that every bone in his body and every exaggerated movement he made shrieked with the repugnance of striking arrogance. He demanded attention from everybody in the courtroom, flaunting his position as the top governmental authority in this case. At the same time, however, he desperately attempted to convey an absolute nonchalance regarding this case and the fact that everything about it was just a waste of his valuable time.

Outwardly, Hill would have been a very intimidating figure for most people. What prevented this for me was a glaring insecurity within him that was so transparent. It was almost as if Hill was a comic figure who had just jumped out from the pages of a comic book. There was nothing comical, however, about the vengeance this prosecutor carried for me or about the resources he had at his disposal to destroy me. It had been almost three years since I had unknowingly challenged and opposed Hill in the courtroom at the Russian Mafia sentencing hearing. I had become his target since that day. The fires had been fueled even more by my repeated refusals of his overtures for a plea bargain.

As we met again face to face, I now recognized a striking scarlet birthmark covering half of his face. With his anger for me boiling underneath the surface, and with the unlimited government agents and resources at his whim, I, along with my family, were expendable because we'd had the audacity to get in his way. I saw his power as an almost insurmountable foe. He made the Russian Mafia members I had so far encountered seem like Boy Scouts. Finally, after almost three years of pent-up resentment, he was meeting face to face with the object of his wrath.

"Are you Dr. Norman?" he asked disinterestedly, fully knowing the answer.

The look in his eyes removed all lingering doubt about why I had been arrested. This was payback. His proud glare spoke volumes to me, conveying, *How did you enjoy that this morning?*

He handed me a forty-five–page indictment outlining all of my supposed crimes against the government of the United States. I was then directed to sit at a long defendant's table, situated on the right side of the courtroom, with all of my new acquaintances whom I had shared a cell with that day. I got the feeling that I stood out with my red knit polo shirt, white Bermuda shorts, and black Sketcher sneakers as I sat next to the rugged and haggard criminals surrounding me. We all sat there, reading our respective indictments, for some time until the judge began to speak.

This was an anxious time for me, for I knew that our bail was about to be set. With Laura and my mother and father seated directly behind me, I took my seat next to the Russian at the table. He had a lawyer present to assist him through this process, and for a moment I felt helpless as I watched him being prepared.

The first question the judge asked was if we all understood the charges and information contained within our indictments. The judge focused on me, as she had noticed each of the other defendants still noticeably struggling to read through the first couple of pages while I had completed a quick scan through all forty-five of my pages. As the other defendants nodded their heads to the judge, I was the first person to speak up. The question I asked was a sign of good things ahead for me.

Without any legal advice or legal schooling or background and after never having laid eyes on this indictment before, my question to the judge went right to the heart of the weakest aspect of the government's case against me. Although I did not realize the crucial nature of my question at the time, I did sense an uneasiness and a respect coming from the other table of prosecutors as I asked it.

After noticing the individual listing and description of each of the counts of the indictment, I had noticed my name listed only twice in the entire forty-five pages, even though I was being charged with ten federal counts. These counts included conspiracy to commit mail fraud, federal perjury, and eight individual counts of mail fraud. *In other words, why was I in the courtroom that day?*

"Judge, I am confused because I am being charged with ten counts but I can only find my name listed twice within the entire indictment," I said respectfully.

The judge turned toward the prosecutors and asked Hill to explain. With an admirable tap dance around the question, he made his vow to the judge. "Judge, it will be tied together later," he said, using his best disinterested, matter-of-fact tone.

I learned later that this was also the explanation that had been given to the grand jury to obtain the indictment in the first place. Hill and his agents had applied their full court press and offered their version of the truth to these unsuspecting men and women on the grand jury. I learned later that Playdoh, my border collie, could have just as easily been indicted based on these tactics.

In the months that followed, it became very apparent that Hill had a difficult time answering this question because he had never intended to include me on the indictment as a member of the conspiracy in the first place. In regard to the Russian Mafia's health care fraud, the government was obligated to respond and bow to the pressure exerted on them by the health insurance companies and their attorneys, who were waging their multimillion-dollar civil suit to recover false medical claims and avoid paying future claims. The Russians' illegal activities equated to millions of dollars of insurance company money, and if a doctor was implicated, the insurance companies' case would be a slam dunk. Working closely with the insurance companies' civil case, Hill's strategy all along had been to pressure me into a guilty plea before the case even started and to coerce me to become his star government witness against anybody and everybody he wished to destroy. I just could not shake the fact that my family and I were mere pawns caught up in this cruel process.

"Dr. Norman, is your understanding sufficient to proceed?" the judge asked.

"Judge, since being taken into custody this morning, I have not been allowed to make any phone calls or contact an attorney. I don't know exactly what I am supposed to do," I replied honestly.

It was at that time that I actually felt as if the judge began to sympathize with me and helped me as best she could. She explained that this was just a formality hearing and that I was probably okay without an attorney. She then asked all of the defendants if they owned passports. I was the only one to raise my hand, and she explained that I would have to surrender it. And then, finally, the judge asked the prosecutors what they recommended for bail in each of our cases.

As it came to my turn, I held my breath and anxiously clenched my fist.

"PRB, your honor," Hill replied.

I instantly felt the relief upon hearing that statement. All I knew was that a personal recognizance bond (PRB) meant I would be going home and Laura and I would not have to mortgage our home to raise bail money.

After my arraignment, I was taken back to the jail to retrieve my belongings and was instructed to meet with my probation officer for the first time. My probation officer and I talked about the conditions of my release, and she stated that she would stop by my home that evening to collect my passport. I was now under the watchful eye of the government; all of my movements would be monitored. I even learned that if I left my county and crossed over its boundary line without permission, I would risk going back to prison until my trial. The loss of freedom is a painful state to live in.

At the conclusion of that parole meeting, I rejoined my family, who were awaiting me, and we left the courthouse. I drove home with Laura, and for the first time all day, I felt like I had rejoined the human race. Even though it had been just one day, it was a strange feeling to go back into my old life after having inhabited a foreign parallel universe. I left behind its iron bars, concrete fortresses, and the permeative atheistic humanism that ruled that world. I wanted never to return again. Laura and I rode home and talked about where and how she had received the news that day and her conversation with the government in her frantic attempts to locate me. What a memorable first day of work she'd had that day!

I arrived back home alone, after Laura went to her mother's house to pick up Madison. As soon as I entered our home, I saw the ironing board still out with my clean shirt on it. I looked at that site nostalgically, remembering that simple morning activity as my last undertaking before my life had taken a radical change. I went into the bedroom and let Playdoh out of her cage, where she had been locked all day because of my arrest. I collapsed upon my bed and closed my eyes.

The silence was interrupted thirty minutes later by my doorbell and Playdoh's barking. For a second, I got a terrible feeling, but then I remembered my probation officer was going to pay me a visit. This would be the first of many unexpected home and office visits that would take place over the next year. If any circumstance of these visits was not to her liking, I would quickly find myself back in prison. This is why I cordially greeted her like an old friend.

Over the next year, this cordiality had to be extended on many occasions, including a home Christmas decoration inspection to ensure I was not a flight risk. Some months later, we would meet again for an early morning encounter on my front lawn as she handed me my morning newspaper. Today, she was here for my passport, and I went to the door to hand it over and we wished each other a good evening.

* * *

What happened next that day was a small glimpse of the extraordinary gift that would come into my life over the course of the next year. This gift was an unexplainable and ever-increasing strength and peace that would permeate my life and our family and one that had been steadily building since my plunge into the sacramental life of Catholicism. I call it a gift because I did not ask for it or consciously perform any activity to create it. It simply was bestowed upon me from a gracious and loving God, who seemed well pleased that I was doing His will.

I calmly but hastily got dressed, got in my truck, and went to the 7:00 p.m. parents' meeting at Madison's new school, where she would start kindergarten in two days. As I sat in the audience that night, meeting other parents and listening to the teachers and administrators for the upcoming school year, the nightmare of the day's events became a distant memory. The true priorities of life became glaringly apparent as I sat among those 150 parents discussing the curriculum, upcoming field trips, and new experiences that were about to fill the lives of our kindergarten children. That evening, there was no other place I desired to be.

I unsuccessfully tried to hold back a huge smile on my face as I looked around the room at the faces of many of the other parents. The momentousness of this occasion was lost on many of them as the noticeable stress and fatigue from their long day was clearly evident. A 7:00 p.m. Monday-night parents' meeting for kindergarten was probably the last place they wished to be. I wondered if anybody in that room had just experienced a day such as mine as I laughingly thought, *You have no idea!*

My life was in absolute ruin, and I had no idea what my next step would be. Still, within my situation of hopelessness, I had the most incredible underlying feeling of calm, peaceful surrender to what lay ahead for me. My past tendency to always attempt to control events of my life was now long gone. The loving embrace of this calm peacefulness was being exerted down upon me from some other place. It did not remotely come from any effort of mine. I went home that night and tightly held Laura and Madison for a long time. Then I drifted off to the deepest sleep I had experienced in many months.

Defeat Fear

Fear derails more people from their purpose and mission than almost any other hurdle. Fear is a miserable self-imposed prison, and it is the devil's greatest weapon against us. It affects every part of life, including relationships, health, mind, and soul. Fear is the enemy of eternity and is not compatible with our docility to the Holy Spirit. In Scripture, we are repeatedly commanded by Christ to defeat fear and increase our faith. Our Lord taught us that the plan of salvation cannot be achieved in the presence of fear.

To defeat fear, we must live for eternity and keep our eyes on the prize. Fear cannot easily derail us as we consider that ten billion years is less than one second in eternity! No passing fear in this life must jeopardize missing out on this. Each day, life advances and eternity approaches. How are we spending our days? If we must fear something, in the words of St. Augustine, "fear the graces of God never to return again." Or, after our eighty years of life have drawn to a close and we find ourselves facing God and recounting how we spent our days, *fear the possibility that all of our work could have been accomplished in a mere decade and we wasted the remainder of our years.* As we stand before God's tremendous judgment seat, no one will be able to answer for us.

To defeat fear, we must reject comfort and embrace growth. Comfort comes as a guest, stays to host us, and enslaves us for the rest of our lives. We must reject comfort and be careful not to fear pain and suffering. All growth and everything we desire reside just outside of our comfort zones...even God (Rev 3:16). We have to get comfortable being uncomfortable and have to be willing to feel awkward. We are asked to jump into a muddy pond despite not knowing how deep or what may reside under the surface. But we must jump anyway.

To defeat fear, we must create massive goals. It is fear that prevents us from thinking big, so each of us must work hard to develop an immense vision for life with crystal-clear clarity. The excitement and energy behind a vision such as this is contagious. Huge goals inspire others to want to play and force us to grow to achieve them. We effectively stretch our zone of competence and step out into a zone of incompetence. In so doing, one of two things will happen: either we attract others to help us or we force ourselves to grow and get competent. Either way, although things may come and go, we win, and who we become during this process can never be taken away from us.

Finally, to defeat fear, we must always keep our eyes on the cross. As Christians, we lose courage and are derailed from our purpose and mission because we do not consistently look to the cross and upon the One we have pierced. The cross is at the center of our universe and is the way God chooses to unite with us. We must not lose sight of the agony He endured for our sake. It requires of us a constant surrendering with our lives as we look for every opportunity to unite our pain and suffering in this life with His pain and suffering.

Throughout history, only a small group of people have ever changed the world. Many souls have sadly held back their contributions to humanity out of fear. They were afraid of unknown waters, so they stayed in the mediocre waters of the shallow end. Inhibitions starve history and are destructive; they do not come from an uninhibited Creator. By contrast, the uninhibited make history and are creative and constructive, guided by the Holy Spirit.

True freedom shall only come to us in the uninhibited service of good and truth. Feel the fear and take one more step! It doesn't last long. Live each day as if it is your last. In the end, the devil is a coward and always backs down from a good fight.

CHAPTER SEVEN:

Friends, Foes, and Fools

"Jesus proclaims that life finds its center, its meaning and its fulfillment when it is given up. We too are called to give our lives for our brothers and sisters, and thus to realize in the fullness of truth, the meaning and destiny of our existence."

Pope John Paul II

I AM CONVINCED THAT GOD introduces people into our lives for an intended purpose and by so doing, if we remain open to His will, pushes us all a little closer to our true destinies. This was certainly true regarding our eventual criminal defense attorney, Jim. Jim is the hardest-working attorney I have ever met, and the year we spent together in preparation for our trial created a bond that we will carry the rest of our lives.

A former prominent district attorney, Jim exemplified a true Southern gentleman in every sense of the word. Upon our first meeting, I instantly felt as if I had met Atticus Finch from Harper Lee's *To Kill a Mockingbird*. Tall, thin, and with a booming voice that made me feel the passion of his emotions, Jim held firm to his conservative values, loyalty, and old-fashioned work ethic. As it so rarely does in our day and age, Jim's word and handshake still represented something to be honored and protected, just as it had with Atticus.

Jim was a strong Catholic family man with past aspirations for the seminary. He proudly displayed a framed portrait of St. Thomas More in his conference room that made me feel as if we were being watched as we worked. Just like More's, Jim's integrity and readiness to take a principled stand for truth and justice, despite the costs, stood out. All of this made him a rare commodity among his colleagues. Laura and I discovered this the hard way because Jim was not among the initial attorneys we worked with.

The event that led to the hiring of our first attorney was that dreadful phone call by Agent Hennessey on May 1, 1997. After awakening from that nap with Madison and being told I would be indicted in two weeks, I had been rendered useless upon our living room sofa. With her frantic calls all over the city, Laura had finally arranged an appointment with an attorney named Riley. This appointment was based solely upon the fact that he was the only one who didn't immediately refuse our case or laughingly attempt to convince us of the absolute hopelessness of our situation.

Our first meeting with Riley the following day at our home, which was filled with family members for support, was memorable. As Riley arrived, we were concluding our meal of delivered pizza, and Laura, my father, and I cleared a spot for him at the kitchen table. My first impression was that Riley was a young, clean-cut, and pleasant person who said all the right things to comfort us. Even though hints surfaced that he was an inexperienced attorney, Riley was the only semblance of a life raft for us within this nightmare. We hung on tightly, and I proceeded to spill my guts and tell him all the facts of the case.

At the conclusion of my story, Riley awkwardly asked Laura and I what we were able to pay him. I told him I had four thousand dollars in my business account, and he said that would be fine. I wrote him a check, and he left.

At that particular time, I was expecting to be indicted in two weeks as Agent Hennessey had assured me over the phone that I would be. As this deadline passed, my new attorney began to receive intentionally cruel telephone calls from Hennessey, indicating that the indictment should be forthcoming any day now. The early weeks and months of that twenty-eight month period are painful to remember, as the pressure mounted and I was increasingly smothered with a cloud of uncertainty, stress, and anxiety. This miserable feeling was further compounded by the actions directed at me by my first attorney.

Very early after our first meeting, Riley had obviously set his mind on obtaining a plea bargain from the government for me, despite my objections. Although I could never be certain, I feel that he had communicated to Hill from day one that he could deliver me with a guilty plea. I had no idea at the time how common this is with criminal defense attorneys who have no desire to see the inside of a courtroom in defense of their clients. I presupposed that my attorney's motives were to seek leniency, but I began to see another motive surface as well.

Occasionally, it is heard that a legal client has deep pockets. Laura and I were the complete opposite of this. Unknown to us, Riley had decided to make the best of the situation. With very little effort, he could simultaneously siphon off the last of our meager resources, gain acceptance and approval as an up-and-coming defense attorney, and ingratiate himself with the federal prosecutor for his future cases. How fortunate it was that he had stumbled upon this high-profile and publicity-producing case.

Riley constantly hounded and badgered me into pleading guilty and frequently got upset when I insisted upon my innocence and my desire to fight this case. I recall one occasion when he phoned my home at night.

"I am not going to hang up until you tell me why we should fight this!" He was proud of himself that he secured a plea bargain for me for felony perjury, and he was shocked I would not take it. "It's only a charge of perjury against you. You need to take this, because technically, you did this!" he angrily responded.

The initial pleasantness and friendliness my family and I had encountered at our first meeting with Riley was now gone. He was out of control. His tantrums and outbursts also extended to his office staff on periodic occasions, when the stress of the case reached particular levels. I remember him losing his head and becoming flustered, especially following phone calls from the government. I had never hired or worked with an attorney before. I assumed all of this was routine within the context of a high-profile case; I did not know any better.

Looking back on it now, however, I see that his tactics seemed to break me down much the same way the government did. He frequently instilled doubt and uncertainty within me, leading me to constantly question myself regarding my guilt or innocence. I actually began to wonder if he was correct and I was truly a criminal after all. Riley's defeatist attitude regarding the prospects of going to trial was infectious. His job was to take clients' money and secure plea bargains.

The tactics Riley used culminated a few months before my arrest. The deadline for the plea bargain he had secured had finally arrived. Hill had promised to take the plea bargain off the table at the end of this particular day. With the daily pressures I endured from Riley to take Hill's various plea deals, I was left very battered and weakened as I contemplated my two choices. These were two life choices a human should not have to make, but the choice was made much more difficult with Riley's pressure tactics.

The first option was Riley's favorite. I could plead guilty to felony perjury, receive probation, avoid prison, and have all other charges against me dropped. "Take this deal! Save your life and don't throw away your family," he urged me day after day.

A small detail in this option was always downplayed by Riley and Hill. The two of them often seemed to team up against me even though I was Riley's client. With this option, I would be required to testify for the government against other targets of their choosing. These would be individuals unknown to me and of whom I would have no knowledge of any wrongdoing. My testimony would be prepared by the government and would be very convincing, most assuredly sending these people to prison for many years.

To receive my reward, I was asked to lie and seal the fate of countless others. I later discovered how common this practice is in our criminal justice system. At the time however, the thought of doing such a thing made me sick inside. I often thought of Matthew 10:39: *"Whoever finds his life will lose it, and whoever loses his life for my sake will find it."*

My second option was a crazy impossibility according to Riley, and one he wasn't sure he would accept and defend at trial if I insisted upon it. Just the mention of this option infuriated him. This was the choice to fight the charges at trial and prove my innocence.

Riley tortured me with stories of prison life. It was drilled into my head that I could not win and would go to prison for at least ten years, losing my wife and daughter. Riley told me how common it was for wives to divorce husbands who made the choice to go to trial and lost. He tried every angle of persuasion upon me, and it took its toll. Frequently overpowering the Matthew verse in my head was an increasingly relentless voice of self-preservation: *Don't be stupid! I have to take the plea for the sake of my family!*

On the deadline day for my decision, I was thoroughly confused and unsure of what to do. The entire future of my family hung in the balance depending on what I would choose, and I was in no shape to make an informed rational decision. I left my office at lunch that day and went down the street to a nearby church. Upon entering, I found a pew and knelt down to pray.

After about fifteen minutes in the silence of prayer, I was given a wonderful insight into my dilemma. I saw myself living out the consequences of each of my potential choices. Like two movies playing simultaneously in my head, I saw how my life would turn out according to which choice I followed.

In one movie, after taking the deal and essentially lying to implicate others for the government, I saw myself alone in the dark. This visual image came with the overwhelming feeling of a hollowed-out emptiness and a miserable void within my soul. Even though I had considered taking this deal only out of fear for losing my family, I could not see or find them anywhere in this cerebral movie.

In the second movie, playing at the same time in my head, I saw myself fighting these charges. Win or lose notwithstanding, I instantly felt at peace with this choice, particularly when compared with the desolate emptiness I felt within the other choice. I recalled the initial staff meeting at the medical clinic several years before when I had ignored, to my detriment, the restless voice within warning me of danger. In this second movie, I knew, no matter what happened, everything would somehow be okay. I now knew what I had to do. I promised myself to honor and trust what I had been given in the silence of God and to go against all of these loud voices to the contrary.

I raced back to my office on that crisp fall day in 1998 and phoned my attorney. I was scared to death of what would now happen. There would be no going back after what I was about to say. I felt like an ant going up against the most powerful force in the world. Most troublingly, this life choice was coming from a mere *voice* in my head. I took a deep breath and uttered the words. "Riley, I've decided to fight this. I didn't do anything wrong. I can't testify against people I don't know and put them in prison. Win or lose, I'm going to fight this. That's my decision. Tell them it's final."

After the longest awkward silence, he responded. "Mike, you're a fool! Just go ahead and throw your life away and jump off a cliff, because that's exactly what you're doing. You're a fool!"

This was our last substantive conversation. Over the next several weeks, my fear was replaced by the familiar calm, peaceful strength that would return to me again and again as my life choices reflected God's will. The wisdom of a most gracious and loving God is always foolishness to men.

* * *

Despite our last confrontation, Riley was still my attorney of record on the morning of August 9, 1999, when federal agents came knocking at my door and took me away to prison. It was on this day that a welcome, and quite probably divine, occurrence took place that would drastically shape the outcome of our ordeal.

As I sat in my prison cell, Riley happened to be out of town and could not be reached. He failed to check in or to return any of our phone calls. This still leaves Laura and me suspicious, as we have never received the full story regarding his absence. However, the fact remains.

As U.S. Attorney Hill orchestrated the events of that morning from his downtown office, Riley chose to sit this one out. The house of Riley's client, an obviously nonviolent white-collar defendant, was raided at gunpoint by six federal agents in full tactical gear in front of the client's five-year-old daughter. His client was then taken into custody, imprisoned, placed before a magistrate for an arraignment hearing, and released into the custody of a probation officer. All this without an attorney who was unavailable that day and not checking messages. This was also in stark contrast with the routine voluntary surrender normally afforded white-collar defendants. Unnerving as Riley's absence was at the time, it was truly a blessing in disguise.

After experiencing Riley's lack of knowledge and dedication to my case, the lack of any advanced warning of my arrest, his continuous defeatist attitude, and now his unexplained absence, I realized that a new attorney was necessary. It is difficult now to understand why I remained under Riley's damaging negative influence for so long. In reality, it was quite simple.

The world we share with six billion other human beings suddenly becomes extremely lonely. Even friends and family members become scarce during these times of trial. When the good guys *and* the bad guys are both trying to destroy you, there are very few places to go.

Laura and I discovered quickly how grown adult attorneys who swore an oath to protect the rights of the innocent shuddered with fear as they considered defending us in this seeming hopelessness. They urged me (if they even bothered to return our calls) to give up and just admit to crimes I had not committed. Government agents scrutinized our phone records. My family and I were followed on several occasions. My mother and I were even followed to our favorite Italian restaurant one night. As we nervously ate inside, the feds kept watch over us from a dark Suburban just outside. These same reprisals could also extend to any attorney who chose to stand up and champion our cause.

As you can see, then, when we find somebody who even remotely comes close to taking our side, as Riley did, we tend to keep those people around and overlook any shortcomings. That is why if Riley had bothered to show up on the day of my arrest, I probably would have kept him on as my counsel and made no changes. If that scenario would have played out, however, changes would have ultimately been inevitable. Most assuredly, I would have had to adjust to ten or more years in prison!

* * *

The scales of lady justice are never blind to a pile of money. Financially speaking, we had no possibility of winning within our legal system. The exorbitant legal expenses throughout this entire ordeal appeared insurmountable. These obligations included the legal fees from Riley, but Laura and I were also subjected to legal fees from the very expensive civil suit arising from the Russians' creditors. These fees, however, would all be dwarfed by the monstrous fees that would be necessary for a federal criminal trial against the U.S. government. It might be tempting to infer that a doctor could afford a high-priced legal team, but I can assure you nothing could have been further from the truth!

Laura, Madison, and I lived very simply, having just moved into our small home when I received that infamous May 1, 1997, phone call from the government. Up until that point, Laura and I had lived at several addresses, including various small rental homes and apartments and with Laura's mother, Dee. After getting married, we moved an average of about once a year as we struggled through the initial years of building our lives and a struggling practice.

Following Madison's birth in 1994 and the ensuing life-threatening complications for her and Laura, we had accumulated significant medical bills, which had exhausted the meager savings we did possess. In addition, I was responsible for my monthly federal student loan payments, which accounted for a big chunk of our monthly income. Although our family was happy, we barely subsisted paycheck to paycheck and were in no position to weather the financial storm of legal fees that were headed our way.

During the twenty-eight–month period when we were in legal limbo awaiting an indictment to be handed down, it became increasingly clear to me that I would be forced to work with a court-appointed attorney. In theory, this is a wonderful protection afforded to us by our U.S. constitution, but as I would discover, it was essentially worthless. I had no financial means to pay the legal fees that Riley was estimating it would cost if we went to trial. My parents and Dee were also unable to assist us at this time because of recent changes in their careers and their inability to access their limited company pensions and retirement plans. In addition, I felt very strongly about not putting them through an unfair financial burden that I knew they were in no position to handle.

Financially, this was a very difficult time for us, and we were sickened by the unfairness of this entire ordeal as we saw what the future held for us. The fear and anxiety of this time often gave way to anger. We had done nothing wrong, but it did not matter. Hennessey had fabricated my confession out of thin air, and Hill had run it through the grand jury. Because of this, everything we owned in life was soon going to be taken from us. Worst of all, our family was soon going to be taken away and there was nothing we could do to stop it.

It is frightening to think, but this scenario could happen to any of us at any time. In the coming months, I would be introduced to many low-income individuals caught up in the wheels of the criminal justice system just like me. Many of these individuals were denied justice and equal treatment because financial resources were not available to them. Their lives were forever altered. Our legal and political system within the U.S. is definitely for sale. If one does not have the money to play, the doors of justice are shut in his or her face.

As mentioned earlier, I had decided to hire a court-appointed attorney in the face of a monumental trial against the U.S. government. I was at peace with this decision and felt very strongly that my innocence would allow me to beat the government on its own dime with a court-appointed counsel. Experience would soon teach me that this was truly the thinking of an extremely naïve and idealistic U.S. citizen.

This was still my plan as I was brought before the judge at my arraignment hearing on the day of my arrest. The judge received my court-appointed request and proceeded to look over my file to see if I qualified. Flat broke, with grim prospects of a future livelihood, I was very upset to hear I had to *qualify* for something that was supposedly afforded by the U.S. constitution! I remained silent, however, and let the judge do her job.

The papers and files that she received were the result of a ten-minute jailhouse interview I'd had with an assigned probation officer while in federal lockup. The questions were extremely superficial, asking for such information as my address, employment, estimated income, estimated expenses, and debts. This apparently was all that was necessary to determine if I qualified for something guaranteed in my constitutional rights. The judge took maybe a minute to review this info. Quite possibly all she noticed was the "Dr." before my name.

"Well, it appears you do not qualify for a court-appointed attorney. You will have to provide your own counsel," she informed me.

That was it. Final. End of discussion. Laura and I had no money, but we were expected to hire a criminal attorney who would accept this monstrous case and go up against the most powerful government in the free world in a jury trial that would last God knew how long. If this is happening every day in the United States, our system is irretrievably broken.

＊＊＊

The miracles that would increasingly begin to unfold in our ordeal were not always limited to mere events. They also extended to our overall financial situation. Through a family member, we were introduced to Jim, our new lawyer, who provided us with his fee to accept our case. After we collectively gulped to remove the lumps in our throats, we took a deep breath and set about trying to come up with his fee. Laura and I liquidated everything we had, including IRAs, college accounts, and home furnishings, and took out a home equity loan. Despite all of this, we were still extremely short.

This was when we heard from our families, who selflessly gave of their resources. Laura and I will forever owe them a debt of gratitude. Their individual circumstances began to change from possessing primarily nonliquid assets, unavailable company pensions, and unstable career situations. Floodgates seemed to open, and resources began to burst forth from every conceivable direction. Liquid bonuses were received, pay raises took place, assets became available, and circumstances within both families' careers improved and stabilized. Selflessly and with love, they offered their help to Laura and me.

Together, we were all able to meet Jim's fee. The financial resources we were able to gather, although crippling to our families and ourselves, were nothing short of a miracle. The vastness of this feat and the love ushered forth through family was, and still is, unimaginable.

Laura and I were colossal life losers, according to our bank account and the materialistic standards of the world. At the same time, we knew we were richer than we could ever imagine, for we had a strong, vibrant faith and the certainty that we were following God's will; a close, loving family who believed in each other and stood united against this injustice; and now, a principled attorney who believed in our innocence and would walk through hell with us.

A few weeks later, I celebrated my birthday. To mark the occasion, Laura and I could only afford a trip to our local 7-Eleven to get matching Big Gulps. Regardless, we could not help but smile and laugh together on our austere date, as the realization of our blessings were unmistakably apparent to us. As we faced a most difficult year ahead, the preparation had begun for our fight to expose the truth of this case and surrender to God's plan regarding the outcome.

Trust His Voice and Accept Help from Others

When the voices of our souls have more influence on us than all the voices on the outside, we have become very close to mastering our lives. We no longer are concerned about becoming fools before others. The closer we get to Christ, the less our feelings can become hurt, even in the face of humiliations and embarrassments. At such a stage, we even become crazy or foolish enough to think we can change the world. However, when the voices on the outside come from those with great influence over us such as family, friends, advisors, and teachers, this endeavor becomes much more difficult and painful.

St. Thomas More once wrote, "Jesus is the paradigm for all martyrs." He referred, of course, to the fact that we should look to Christ to imitate in the midst of trials, because Christ has already experienced everything that may come our way. More would eventually rely on such wisdom more than he could have imagined when he found himself imprisoned in the Tower of London and awaiting execution for refusing to sign King Henry VIII's oath of succession, stemming from the king's immoral marriage. As More sat in his cold jail cell, just a few months removed from being the second most powerful man in England, the king permitted visitors to the Tower in attempts to sway More's conscience.

Alice, More's wife, visited one day and attempted to dissuade his stand by stressing the luxurious comforts of his estate compared to his small, dark, cold jail cell. On another occasion, More's beloved daughter, Margaret, who had already signed the oath, came to visit and to convince her father to save his own life. She used the familiar and admirable wit and rational logic the two legal minds had shared between them for years. Their brief time together brought back a flood of emotion to More's soul.

These outside voices of influence on our lives cut like knives to our very core and cause the voices of our own souls to waver and falter. We begin to internally question our stances as futile folly, or even as just stubborn, arrogant pride. Only through great strength and conviction can we, like More, hold true to our consciences and the voice of God speaking within our souls.

St. Thomas More's strength of conscience came largely from his understanding of the Mystical Body of Christ and the communion of souls shared between the living and the dead. As we gain this understanding also, we discover that our covenant family is so much bigger than we could ever imagine. Going far beyond the visible world, Christ's Mystical Body is composed of one big interconnection of the living, the dead, the saints, the souls in purgatory, and the souls in Heaven. We simply have to ask its members, our brothers and sisters in Christ, who possess every different talent, gift, and charism, and assistance becomes freely available to any of us at any time. To separate the living and the dead by viewing Christ's Body as merely the visible church on Earth is tragic.

To deny our connection to our deceased brothers and sisters in Christ and their desire to intercede on our behalf is the reason many Christians fail to carry Christ into our world with supernatural strength and courage. Christ knows we cannot accomplish His will alone. From the beginning, His will has been accomplished through humankind. For His will to usher forth and His graces to be transferred in this world, Jesus uses His *entire* Mystical Body, living and deceased. As one large supernatural interconnection of souls united to Him, we become His instruments. He desires His instruments to connect and to lift up other family members with the gift of our lives. If we ignore this fact, we will someday wake up to find we have lived self-absorbed shells of existence.

We are surrounded by family. The saints in Heaven are urging us on Earth to live our lives boldly and with courage. Likewise, the souls in Purgatory are urging us on Earth for our strength and our prayers. Simultaneously, we have great support *from*, as well as a great responsibility *to*, our brothers and sisters in Christ. They exist side by side with us as we experience the victories, struggles, and challenges of this life as we endeavor to usher forth Christ's kingdom here on Earth. We would never have occasion to fear again if we truly knew who walks beside us in every moment!

As we follow the voices of our own souls, despite the cost, we should never fear becoming fools before others. This massive family of souls, having already run their races, proudly look on, intercede, and urge us to fight the good fight and finish the races that lay ahead of us. Our brothers and sisters within the Mystical Body will be there with Christ to welcome us home at the finish line. Unlike the voices of fear in our world today, our covenantal family shall never view one who follows God's voice as a fool.

To carry Christ into our world, we must live lives of choices rather than lives of reactions. With the help of our extended family, God's voice in our soul becomes more recognizable. God's voice within us surfaces from deep within the peace of our souls and is never the voice that comes out of a state of fear, anger, haste, or any other crisis reaction on our part. Such reactions require no thought or choice on our part and do not come from the Holy Spirit. Sadly, much of our world resides within this crisis mode of initial human reaction, rooted in fear, doubt, and self-preservation.

Rather, God's voice will always involve our thoughts and choices in the process. In the midst of great trial, when we need God's voice and direction most, we must be willing to listen. By pulling back and waiting for our initial human reactions to pass, taking a deep breath, praying, and asking our brothers and sisters within Christ's Mystical Body for help, we always receive guidance about the proper choices for our lives.

God's voice from the peace of our souls always takes the risk on the side of love and always chooses hope. Ultimately, in time, God's voice becomes amplified to the point of drowning out the outside voices of our world. This is how we can hold our heads up high with hearts filled with hope during the darkest storms of our lives. This is also how St. Thomas More came to bless his executioner with his final words as he faced the king's guillotine.

CHAPTER EIGHT:

Gethsemane

"This (dark night) guided me more surely than the light of noon."

St. John of the Cross

THE WORD "GETHSEMANE" MEANS "THE place of the (olive) oil press. This place where Christ was squashed in agony before his crucifixion is a place where we all find ourselves on occasion. When we experience our times in Gethsemane, the pain and agony that accompany it can be greater than any crucifixion to follow.

This is true because Gethsemane can bombard our wills with extreme emotions of self-doubt, fear, anguish, anxiety, and the ceaseless second-guessing of ourselves and our situations. After deciding to fight the indictment, I thought, *Am I being stubborn, unreasonably prideful, or insane? Is this unfair to my family? Is this a foolish battle I invented in my own head that will land me in prison unnecessarily? Is this some futile stand that won't make any difference whatsoever?* Our heads constantly churn with thoughts like these in Gethsemane.

Worse yet, as previously mentioned, these thoughts and fears are reinforced as we become extremely susceptible to the suggestions and opinions of others because of our weakened states. When we are in Gethsemane, we must be ready for the many individuals, with their varying mixtures of motives and desires, who will attempt to provide easier roads to travel and convince us to avoid our sufferings at all costs. A vast spectrum of individuals present formidable obstacles in

Gethsemane—from our well-intentioned loved ones who can't bear to witness our pain, to a secular society armed with a superficial faith and a limited capacity for suffering, and, finally, to the ever-present wolves of deception that can surround us. Sensing our weakness, these wolves move in on their vulnerable prey with soft words and outward smiles but with malice and exploitation in their hearts.

It is most striking, in contemplation of Christ's passion, just how many opportunities He had to turn away from His sufferings and to alter His mission. The strength He exhibited is incomprehensible. He followed through with the will of the Father despite His ability to call down legions of angels and to conform events according to human will. After Christ's ministry of strengthening others, His weakest hour was at Gethsemane, and the temptations that surfaced there had to be close to overwhelming.

Following my release from prison and the hiring of our attorney Jim, it was time to take the next step. We had to appear before the judge in my case to enter a formal plea. After we had entered my plea, a trial date would be set and we could begin the extensive preparation necessary to undergo a federal criminal trial. Although not completely aware of it at the time, I was given a sign of things to come at this hearing.

As Jim and I waited in the courtroom for our turn to enter a plea, we viewed a seemingly endless line of defendants and their attorneys, unrelated to my case, appearing before the judge. Being new to the criminal justice system, I was struck with the efficient, routine, and businesslike nature of these proceedings by everybody involved. Without emotion or very little discussion between judge, attorney and bailiff, each of the lives of these defendants, who were mainly pleading guilty, were being determined within a matter of seconds and then shuffled away to make room for the next one. It was obvious that the defendants' past life choices have caused them to relinquish all control over their lives. Their power of choice was now greatly diminished as they were forced to submit to the authority before them. This was sad, but, even worse, I now found myself among them.

Our turn finally arrived, and Jim and I walked up to the podium to address the judge. The judge finished his paperwork before him and looked up, making initial eye contact with me. I can only explain this first look and reaction from him as the most obvious double-take ever seen. He was obviously struck by the *un-criminal-like* nature of the defendant now before him, and it took him a few brief seconds to regain his thoughts and continue the proceeding.

"Michael Norman, how do you wish to plead?" the judge asked me.

I wanted desperately to explain to the judge everything that was happening to us and how I was not supposed to be there. Instead, I wisely followed Jim's advice.

"Not guilty, Your Honor," I resolutely proclaimed, hoping he could read my mind.

As I looked him sincerely in the eyes, he stared at me silently for a moment. It was almost as if he wanted the explanation about why I was standing there in his courtroom that day. Throughout his endless courtroom days of dealing with a daily procession of guilty pleas and repeat felons, I just did not fit his image. This was the start of things to come.

To make our difficult task even more challenging, the judge set our court date only six months away. When he mentioned the date, February 7, 2000, it may as well have been my execution date. In my mind, as I went home that day, I had six months to live and each day was a step closer to my D-Day. My Gethsemane had now begun. It does not become real until our appointed time has been set. The time would be short, and it would quickly draw near.

I began working with Jim on Tuesdays, Saturdays, and Sundays in grueling marathon sessions that would leave me exhausted and drained. The boxes of documents and files related to my case were mind-boggling, and I had no idea how we were going to get through all of them in just six short months. The stress and anxiety of these sessions provided occasions for flared tempers and heated arguments between Jim and me; however, these periodic occasions only seemed to develop a special chemistry between us, unlike the defeatist tactics and tantrums of my first attorney, which had only served to break me down and weaken my resolve.

As Jim and I began to work tirelessly, preparing for my D-Day, we got to know each other very well. Going beyond the lawyer-client relationship, we became good friends as well. My Atticus Finch first impression proved to be true. Humble and hardworking, Jim possessed a strong moral fabric and integrity that ran through every part of his life. Laura and I were thankful to have found him.

After twenty-five years of law practice, Jim was not immune to a progressive frustration and discouragement with our legal system. After the zeal and passion of law school graduation fades, any honorable attorney will begin to experience this reality as clients and the system increasingly let him or her down. This was when I had met

Jim. As we worked together, I felt his passion for law being reignited. A fire was lit among his entire office staff once again, and even his own family joined us as we prepared to wage this monumental battle. I will always remember Jim's booming, deep Southern drawl, which could be heard throughout the office.

"I didn't think I had another rodeo left in me. Mike, this is why I went to law school!"

When I was not working with Jim, I was approaching February 7, 2000, by living each day of freedom as if it were my last. Although I was certainly not a pessimistic defeatist in attitude, I was willingly surrendering to the will of God. Although subtle as it may be, there is a difference. The more I surrendered to His will, which I felt was calling me to lay down my life and submit to a lengthy prison term, the more peace and strength I felt. In turn, my family felt this peace and strength as well. My biggest concern at that time was not prison, but that weakness would eventually overcome me and I would give in to the government, going against what I knew to be God's will. My prayers for continued strength were constantly under attack, and at times, I was hanging on by a mere thread.

One of the biggest blessings of my ordeal was that it forced my family and me into living each day as if it were our last. It becomes a blessing, because when you have to live in this manner for any length of time, you begin to get used to it as a way of life. Life's priorities become amazingly clear, and the intensity of the experiences sear them into your consciousness in ways you will never forget.

Precious time with family was cherished during this period, and I frequently left Jim's office to spend the lunch period at Madison's kindergarten. Without her knowing, I sometimes would remain a little longer to watch her play at recess afterward. I could not hold back the floodgate of emotion in thinking I may never get this opportunity again. Games of chess and hours at the park with Madison took on monumental importance for me. I was determined to make every second count.

Although Madison was staying outwardly strong, Laura and I could sense the obvious stress she was feeling. Since the day of my arrest, Madison had experienced panic when the doorbell rang at our home. She would dart into another room to hide. On one occasion, Laura and I were given a deeper glimpse into our five-year-old daughter's thought process. As Laura and Madison lay in bed alone one night, an insightful question arose.

"Momma, are the meanies gonna come to our house and get you too?" she asked innocently.

We were embarrassed because it had never occurred to Laura and me to reassure Madison about this.

During our trial preparation, Jim spoke to both Laura and me in his office, fulfilling his duty to explain the implausibility of winning against the U.S. government in a court case. Less than 1% of all federal defendants are successful at trial. He was obviously making sure Laura was clearly aware and able to accept the eventual outcome of my prison term. What she said in response strongly impacted Jim to continue our fight for truth, convincing him of how special this case was. This also marked one of the many occasions when Laura's strength and love instilled within me the courage to continue fighting by trusting and honoring the will of God.

"You know our chances are not that good," Jim honestly told us, looking only at Laura.

Laura immediately spoke up. "Jim, Mike is the strongest person I have ever known. I don't know anybody else that would do what he is doing. He's holding all of us together. He's standing up for God and the truth, even though he's losing everything, even his family. We did nothing wrong and don't deserve what is happening to us."

Long walks and discussions with Laura were very special at this time, creating memories that would undoubtedly bridge the ten-year gap when I would be going away. Families commonly take one of two courses when confronted with significant crisis or tragedy: either a path of separation or a path of unity. The blessings we received for living each day as if our last served to unite us more than we had ever imagined.

Spiritual growth throughout this period continued to occur as my appointed time drew near. I would begin my day with daily Mass and receiving the Lord in the Eucharist. I was fortified with strength to face the agonizing day ahead. Daily Mass was offered at Madison's school, and we would attend together, making it the absolute highlight of my day. I just hoped that she would remember this as I would through the years I would be away from her. I continued to meet with Father John for biweekly spiritual direction and left these visits further strengthened and resolved to carry out God's will.

Despite the periods of strength and peace I would experience on these occasions, Gethsemane would always return to hound me. I was frequently subjected to undermining influences and opinions from many well-intentioned or ill-intentioned individuals who always seemed to come on the strongest when I was at my weakest. My resolve to follow God's will wavered as loved ones reminded me about what I was giving up and as legal experts tried to convince me of the hopelessness of my situation. Painfully, scores of friends, colleagues, and associates whom I turned to for support scattered from Laura and me. To them, I was tainted, and they ignored and refused to take any of my phone calls.

The overwhelming voice of self-preservation, which emanated from a miserable fear and doubt, would prevail on these occasions. This incessant voice would scream at me to save myself at all costs and not go through with this insane notion of God's will. Over and over it had me wondering, *Is my stand simply an invention of my own making?*

It was during one of these episodes that I was confronted with another dreadful choice to make. Just before Christmas in 1999, two months before trial, Hill called Jim and offered me another plea bargain. Similarly to the previous deal, my decision was due after the holidays on January 10, less than a month before our trial was to start. This timing constituted a common psychological ploy intended to place a heavy emotional weight upon a defendant's mind throughout what should be a joyous holiday period with family. Torturously, it worked.

As Jim related the specifics of the plea agreement over the phone, I felt the last remaining ounces of strength being drained from my body. As I listened silently, I began to resign myself to the fact that it was time to come back down from out of the clouds and agree to the realities of this life-saving deal. As I prepared to spend my last Christmas with Laura and Madison, I was too weak and the fight was just too much.

Two life choices were again placed before me. The first choice was to plead guilty to felony perjury. With such a plea, I could avoid ten or more years in prison if I agreed to sign a factual resume admitting to my crimes. In exchange, I would receive only six months of home confinement with one year of supervised release. It was implied that I could even get better than this depending on my "cooperation." The factual resume would state that the patients I treated had never been injured, the office staff had fraudulently prepared insurance forms, I had knowingly signed these fraudulent medical reports, and I had known all of this during my testimony in court and therefore committed perjury.

I was exhausted, drained, depressed, and ready to give in. With my resolve broken, I told Jim I would sleep on it and be in his office the next day. In my mind, however, I had already decided that I would take the deal. My journal entry on this day reflects my emotional state:

12/3/1999 Today was a very bad day but Laura and I went to the mall and did our Christmas shopping this evening. When I get this low it sure helps to go to a public place and look into the faces of complete strangers. It helps to see that we all have crosses to bear in this world."

* * *

The very next morning, I awoke with a burst of energy that I had not experienced in many weeks. I later realized this energy had nothing to do with me. It was a gift of God's grace and part of the fruit we all receive because of spiritual seeds we have sown. Before the sun came up, I was working out hard on our treadmill at a frantic pace unlike I had in quite some time. As I exercised in the silence of our home and I stared out the window into the darkness, I was given a clarity regarding my future as if I had gone into a trance.

I saw what would happen next if I accepted the government's plea agreement. After agreeing and signing, I would have to submit to another FBI 302 (a staged documented interview) and admit to my factual resume with a "cooperative enthusiasm" that would earn me a lesser sentence. I would have to admit that the sham IRS/Secret Service interview was correct and corroborate their preconceived version of events. As I began to run even faster on the treadmill, I saw how I would be openly sued for restitution by the insurance companies for the millions of dollars stolen by the Russians. And, worst of all, I would be expected to testify in court against others, including other doctors, lawyers, secretaries, and office personnel, based on these admissions despite having no knowledge of their wrongdoing. Just like the previous plea agreement, to save myself, I would have to send these individuals to prison with my words.

Although the government insisted my testimony should only be truthful, I was expected to eagerly corroborate their story or my plea bargain would be voided. As I again increased my treadmill speed, this clarity of vision continued. I saw and experienced my entire future filled with incredible regret and worthlessness after lying for my plea bargain and then sitting at home to serve my reward of home confinement. Just like two years before, consideration of this life choice left me with a hollowed-out feeling in my soul. I felt an absolute loss of control over my life and a failure to give God the chance to work His good.

Immediately after finishing my workout, I could hear Laura stirring in the other room after awakening. I walked up to her and said, "Laura, I'm fighting this!"

Laura's face lit up, and we hugged. The mercy of God never leaves us down for long. Although I had wavered greatly, I felt my strength and resolve return to me. Later that morning in Jim's office, after I informed him of my decision, I also felt the fight come back into him as well. I gave him our new motto, which had come to me on the treadmill that morning: *Ten years with honor instead of a lifetime of regret*! For me, this lifetime of regret would then be cruelly followed by the realization that I will someday stand before God. What could possibly be my reply on that day?

What followed over the next several months was a steady succession of important dates and deadlines, but my inward strength and peace endured. The holidays passed that year and left many special memories. The shift into Y2K also passed uneventfully, despite all the dire predictions. Also passing silently was January 10, 2000, the deadline for taking the plea bargain. The date of this once-tormenting decision came and went silently with no call from the government. That left just one more date, D-Day, February 7, 2000, my trial date.

* * *

Cruelly, after a mad flurry of activity by Jim and me and hours of grueling trial preparation, we received a simple phone call from the government just a few days before trial. My trial would be postponed six months until August 7, 2000. *How could they do this? We had prepared for so long and so intensely, to the point of physical exhaustion, for one particular date on the calendar. Now that date is suddenly postponed by the government?* There was a small hint of relief on my part, but mainly, I felt depression, hopelessness, and fatigue. These emotions smothered me after we had done all this work and then had the enemy disregard that sacred date. Another six months! This was complete torture. It felt like the government held our puppet strings and could utilize this delay tactic perpetually at its whim.

The emotional roller coaster of highs and lows can be the most difficult part of an ordeal such as this. Just when we think we are garnering some sense of momentum and strength, our legs are swiftly taken out from under us and we feel like we have returned to square one. This is incredibly draining and exhausting, and the temptation to quit sometimes becomes overwhelming. How difficult it becomes to keep putting one foot in front of the other and hold your head up for another sunrise.

Every now and then, however, in various forms, we are given tiny morsels of inspiration during our low periods. These gifts encourage us to face another day and continue the fight. Although I received countless examples of these inspirational gifts throughout our ordeal, in the form of books, tapes, movies, and nature, I remember a particular source of great strength during this disheartening chapter. After this trial delay, I had a sleepless night that I decided to spend reading. I came across a passage written in 1927 by a Catholic nun named Sister Josefa Menendez in her book *The Way of Divine Love*. This seemingly obscure passage spoke incredibly clear to me that night. It provided just the right encouragement for me to regain my momentum and strength, realigning my embattled perspective as the war waged on:

> When you suffer it is Jesus who reposes in you, so what is there to fear? Abandon yourself to His will. You cannot imagine now what your joy will be for all eternity in heaven, when you see the many souls saved by your little acts and sacrifices. Life is of no account, and yours will pass like a flash! Use every moment of it to merit, by giving your heavenly Bridegroom the glory of complete surrender to His good pleasure. Live in His peace and love, and above all leave Him free to use you.

Our time in this world is truly brief, but the meritorious work we can accomplish in our few years is eternal. I had decided that these next six months would be different than the last, and I made good on this promise. I forged ahead on several personal projects that had been wrongly put on hold. Initially, it feels like we have to forcibly push ourselves back into our projects, but it absolutely must be done.

The absolute temptation to quit on life is tremendously overwhelming in Gethsemane. The enemy follows us wherever we go. The enemy must be fought and defeated at all costs.

By choosing this path, I took the opportunity to coach Madison's six-and-under girls' softball team, which I had contemplated not doing. Instead, I decided there was really nothing else I would rather do. I began to rebuild my neglected practice and expanded my community volunteer efforts, which had wrongly been set aside.

After Christ's time of agony, temptation, and anguish in Gethsemane was complete, He serenely and calmly returned to His disciples. In a strong, confident decisiveness, He rallied them: Get up, get ready and let's go! (Mk 14:42)

The time we spend in Gethsemane encompasses the worst type of pain: protracted mental anguish. However, it will also create one of the greatest transformations within us, if we allow it. We can become strong, decisive, confident moral leaders, shaped by our experiences, who can inspire others around us. Our world desperately needs this right now. This is true even if what lies ahead shall be very hard and filled with frightening uncertainty.

The Nature and Beauty of Christian Suffering

As Christian faithful, it is no accident that the symbol of our faith is a cross, a humiliating instrument of torture, rather than a triumphant flag. Christ did not save us on Palm Sunday by His triumphal ride into Jerusalem with honors. We are saved because of a much darker day on Golgotha after all the cheers and waving palm branches had fallen silent. We would never have had the saving redemptive grace of Easter Sunday without a dark, cloudy Good Friday two days earlier.

If we are in Christ, suffering and salvation shall always go hand in hand. To separate or avoid either of the two removes all purpose from and reason for our existence. We see frequent attempts at both of these approaches in our world today by false prophets with soft messages. The tragic approach of human suffering without salvific merit is pain without the promise. Such an approach is not united with Christ and soon deteriorates into hopelessness and despair. Equally tragic is the assurance of salvation through the avoidance of suffering. A reward without struggle robs life of meaning and leads to the self-destructive results of swollen pride, pursuit of comfort, and self-absorption.

It is always important for us to distinguish between two types of suffering. With painful self-honesty, we must discern between the crosses that God has sent into our lives and the crosses of our own making. There is a question that helps us distinguish between the two: *Are we working to change what can be changed and accepting what cannot be changed?* If the answer is yes, we are walking God's path.

Along with this question, we must ceaselessly pray for His holy wisdom to know the difference. Although God can work through both types of suffering, it remains up to us to take the first step regarding the crosses we have created. These man-made crosses are a result of our choices in life. Quite simply, if we are unwilling to change what can be changed, we must be content to persist in a hell of our own creation until we respond differently.

When we come to know why we suffer, anything

becomes possible. At the center of God's plan of salvation, redemptive suffering requires a supernatural faith and is part of the necessary path to our union with God. This is how God chooses to unite with us. Worldly attachments to our soul must be removed to make room for God. The kingdom of God cannot be ushered in without suffering. As we wake up to this realization, we begin to send ripples out into the sea of eternity.

Regarding suffering in this life, one question remains: Do we have what it takes to choose greatness? Christ faced His suffering head on, although the overwhelming temptation to turn away, particularly at Gethsemane, must have reached supernatural proportions. Likewise, at this very instant, millions of souls await our decisions. One person in this life can make an eternal difference.

True greatness shall only be revealed at the Last Judgment, when we all stand together as the Mystical Body and our salvific work is revealed for all to see. Our time to make an eternal difference is short in this life. Soon, our ability to lift the Mystical Body of Christ with the redemptive grace of our courageous and dignified sufferings will pass away. If we miss our opportunities, we may, quite possibly, become dependent upon the actions of others.

The paradox is striking. Our periods of trial and suffering in this life can truly be gifts if we allow them to be. Life's lowest points can bring us our greatest freedom, happiness, and fulfillment. A loving Father prunes the branches of His vines to unleash an abundance of fruit. This fruit is a supernatural love for our brothers and sisters that embraces the inevitable pain in this life for their sake. The human tears shed for this noble purpose become the wine of angels and cause for great joy in Heaven.

With each passing day, eternity is approaching, and millions of souls await our decision on how we shall spend our lives. What will be revealed of our works on the last day? Did we boldly take the cup and drink from it? Did we choose greatness?

CHAPTER NINE:

Fight the Good Fight

"Even to the death fight for truth, and the Lord your God will battle for you."

Sirach 4:28

DURING A DIFFICULT MOMENT WITHIN the twenty-eight–month pre-indictment period, I spontaneously engaged in an action that I would not hastily recommend to anybody. At least not until they are definitely prepared and ready. I certainly was not, but I blindly unleashed the maelstrom anyway.

After a particularly long day of seeing patients at my practice, I locked up and remained seated in the empty dark office. As I was many times during this period, I was worn out both physically and mentally. Without thinking, in equal parts weakness, hopelessness, and naivety, I knelt down and surrendered myself to God's will.

"Father, not my will but Your will be done. I am your willing servant. Use me for what you will. I am ready."

Far deeper than I had ever dared to go, that spontaneous utterance in that empty office that night, represented words that I had long feared to say. As soon as I finished speaking these words, I knew deep down what this would mean. The consequences of this act would equate to my death: the end of the life I had known and the strong likelihood of the painful loss of the people I had loved.

Over time, I learned with difficulty that these words are never to be spoken lightly. It is true this is the only way to our destinies; nonetheless, when we sincerely open this door and surrender to His will, particularly in times of brokenness, we'd better get ready. Our lives will change dramatically.

Initially, it feels as if we are inviting tragedy. Our lives begin to career out of control and turn upside down with increasing trials and sufferings. There is a broader purpose at work, however. God takes it very seriously when His broken servants become humbly receptive, choosing to be lowly instruments for the purpose of ushering forth His greater good. This was our experience. Looking back, I realize that Laura and I were being slowly prepared all along for the path I knew God wanted me to walk. I had desperately wanted to avoid taking this path because of fear and the seeming insanity of it all. Despite this, I accelerated this course of action that night in my office.

Shortly after my vow of surrender, God allowed the floodgates to open. We were presented with a major preparation for the path ahead, as Laura and I endured the $40,000 civil lawsuit. This was waged against us by a major creditor of one of the now-defunct Russian enterprises. After being unable to locate any of the fleeing Mafia members, the creditor had decided to turn his lawsuit solely on me in hopes of recovering his money.

Although this creditor was entitled compensation from the agreements between him and the Russians, I became the only individual with any type of association to the Russians who could be located; therefore, despite the creditor's knowledge of my hourly wage and employee status to the medical clinic, its entire case was reconfigured and reworded to place sole financial responsibility on Laura and me. We were left to prove otherwise.

Even though the facts of this obvious extortion appeared simple to outside observers, we were forced to hire a civil attorney to fight this lawsuit. Legal fees and expenses, which we did not have the money to cover, piled up as we gathered evidence, deposed witnesses, and engaged in fruitless mediation efforts to settle out of court. Finally in the fall of 1998, the case went to trial and an important preparation for things to come began.

At a key point at the onset of this one-day trial, my fear and weariness got the best of me as the creditor's attorney passed a settlement offer over to my attorney and me, promising a quick end to this matter if we agreed to his demand. In the interest of going home without risking or paying for a trial, and with a settlement offer quite lower than the original $40,000, I gave in and accepted.

As the attorneys went to a back room to discuss the settlement, Laura came up and spoke with me at the defense table.

"This is a joke! These guys are crooks and this is extortion. Don't give them a penny. Let's go to trial!

She was continuing to teach me to stand up and fight for myself. Her words strengthened me as she reminded me how miserable I would become if I had to write a check to this creditor for the next five to seven years for money that I did not owe. She reminded me how much more tolerable it would be if I fought this and had my day in court, even if it meant an increase of our legal bills.

With newfound strength, I left her side and quickly went back to my attorney. As they were busy in the midst of their settlement discussions, I shockingly brought their plans to a screeching halt.

"No deal, we are going to fight this!" I proclaimed.

To the dismay of the opposing attorney, who thought he had an easy financial settlement in hand, the trial proceeded and abruptly ended thirty minutes later after the judge disgustingly dismissed the suit in our favor because of an obvious lack of evidence or cause. Laura had seen all of this so much more clearly than I, and she helped me gain significant preparation for things to come. We learned that justice and the enemies of truth will fall hard in battle when the fight is decisively taken to them. As we left the courthouse that day, Laura and I witnessed a sight that had us laughing all the way home. The creditor and his attorney were having a post-trial meeting on the courthouse steps. As they stood nose to nose and yelled loudly at each other, a security guard was forced to step in between them to prevent a fistfight!

A final major preparation for the path I knew God wanted me to take, but for which I still couldn't fathom how, began almost three years before I was ever indicted and arrested. Shortly after the insurance company deposition and my conclusion of employment at the Russians' medical clinic, I began to experience a recurrent dream that would return to me once or twice a month. I have always had difficulty remembering my dreams, but this particular one was so clear and vivid that I knew it must be very meaningful. In retrospect, I saw the life path that I was meant to walk several years in advance. This partial glimpse of my future included a path that I could not and did not want to walk.

After the conclusion of my employment by the Russians, I began to learn of the extent of their criminal activity. This knowledge came from many sources, including civil attorneys, criminal attorneys, federal agents, federal prosecutors, insurance investigators, local police, and newspaper and television reports. Despite all of these voices directed at me outlining the criminal enterprise, I remained absolutely and positively confused. I had seen nothing that resembled what they were telling me.

It was one of the strangest feelings I had ever experienced, as if the entire world had been let in on some secret and nobody had bothered to tell me. I was left outside looking in during this entire ordeal and was surrounded by emotions of intense loneliness and helplessness. As accusations mount, there is an overwhelming temptation to believe all of the different voices leveled against us. It is extremely difficult to continue to believe in ourselves as we begin to actually accept alternative versions of truth determined by others.

Despite the overwhelming tide rising against me, including the betrayal of false friends, I still possessed the peace of being completely unaware of any Russian criminal enterprise during my employment and an assured innocence in the face of the growing list of crimes I was being accused of. At this early stage of the ordeal, I still maintained that faint glimmer of hope that the truth would come out, justice would be served, and everybody could see that I'd had no involvement in this. That is why this recurrent dream I kept having was so scary.

Months before I had even hired my first attorney, this dream began to occur, and it always started the same way. I witnessed myself testifying in a crowded courtroom as the judge, jury, attorneys, and spectators intently listened in. Each dream had me testifying very emotionally and articulately about various aspects of my case. In my dreams, I always had a ready answer for each question, as if the words were just coming to me at the instant they were needed. When I awoke, I often thought of Matthew 10:19: "*When they hand you over, do not worry about how you are to speak or what you are to say. You will be given at that moment what you are to say.*"

Also upon awaking, the realization would frequently set in that there could be no possible way of becoming this person who mustered the strength to endure a major criminal trial in real life. The person I was in this dream occupied such a larger space and realm than who I was at the moment. It was incomprehensible to think that this could occur in real life. When this dream occurred, I thought of it as a miserable nightmare, leaving me filled with dread.

There was one part of this dream, however, that was more comforting than the rest. Periodically, I would see myself walking down the aisle of the courtroom after hearing the jury pronounce me not guilty. This would not be included in my dream every time. I particularly remember it during the times of my ordeal when I was at my lowest. I would awake with hope, and it always helped me keep going.

Looking back now, I realize I was clearly being led. The events, people, and layout of the courtroom in my dreams were eerily similar to the actual events, people, and layout of the real courtroom four years later. This was God's path, despite all the legal experts who urged me to plead guilty, the seemingly absolute power and invincibility of the U.S. government, the tremendous financial crush upon my family, and the nightmarish possibility of being taken away from Laura and Madison for the next ten years.

In the face of these overwhelming obstacles, I used to wake up in fear, wondering how I could ever live up to and become the person I was in my dreams. I now found myself stepping into the real-life courtroom on August 7, 2000, for the first day of my federal criminal trial. As I heard the menacing words announcing the *United States versus Michael Norman*, I thanked God that I had somehow managed to become just that person.

* * *

8-6-2000   The day is at hand. My time has come to prove that I am worthy to be tested by the fire. What we do in this short life will echo through eternity. I am at peace. I have already lost myself and have picked up my cross and I am lifting it up to glorify the Master. I have no regard for my life any longer. "Whoever tries to save his life shall lose it, but whoever gives up his life for my sake shall find it."

I see today that when we find ourselves in the Heavenly Kingdom, we are absolutely unconcerned and un-remindful of the trials and circumstances of the life we just completed. The kingdom of paradise will have that effect on us. I welcome that day.

Everybody is with me now, in this world and the next. I can feel them all and I am currently an open vessel that they are communicating with. My conscience and inner voice is so loud right now that it is alarming. I couldn't turn it off now if I wanted to.

I am climbing a mountain of such incredible heights that would never have been possible before, if not for the trial which is pushing me there. If this is what it takes to get me to the mountaintop, I gladly welcome it.

Thomas Merton writes that truly great souls always attract an equally competent opponent. He says this is absolutely necessary to push the soul into the creation it was intended to become by the Father. The opponent is absolutely necessary and we must absolutely welcome it!

Laura and Madison are staying very strong because I am staying strong. When families encounter the test, they can either crumble, fall apart, pull away, or they can grow closer into a new creation. I thank God my family falls under the latter category.

When I read that journal entry, written the night before my trial began, I can still feel the intense, heightened anxiety of that time. These last words of mine before the August 7, 2000 trial start date, remind me of how I saw this as my execution date. I had surrendered to the hopeless outcome that lay ahead of me and forcibly pushed myself to take this walk through the fire. The words of this journal entry may today appear as the ramblings of a lunatic, but on that night, they were the vivid speech and thoughts of one who faced his impending death the next day. When all of us come face to face with our own deaths, our speech becomes extremely vivid and we make it a point to not waste any words!

As Jim, Laura, and I walked into the federal courtroom on that first day, I instantly recognized the familiar cast of characters seeking to extinguish our lives. Clearly center stage, U.S. Attorney Hill assured all in the courtroom of his importance within this proceeding by his arrogant demeanor and nonchalant speech. Beside him, also seated at the prosecution table, were two more familiar faces.

After having received the judge's permission, IRS Agent Hennessey, with his perpetual sinister smirk, and FBI Agent Stone, with the perfectly coifed hair, would be present for every day of testimony. They were in rare form and anxious to begin. Over the next three weeks, their exaggerated body language and facial expressions, emphasizing each and every trial point, would attempt to sway court and jury opinion against me. This would also include frequent glances by the agents back at Laura in her first-row seat, offering a whispered threat and an arrogant smile and wink, in regard to the impending demise of her husband.

I also met another character upon entering the courtroom. I finally met, face to face, the real object and source of all of the pain, anguish, and temptation that had constricted my life over these past six years. This opponent was larger than any one person, however; rather, it was an entire system of evil that had completely enveloped me, beginning with the deceit and greed of the Russian Mafia and ending with the deceit and arrogance within the federal government.

Although for much of my life I was unaware of a personified force of evil, I could now instantly recognize him. The devil is real. He was there that day and ready for trial. The repugnant aura was palpable the minute we entered the courtroom.

I felt very small that first day in the courtroom as I faced the full fury and force of this secular and humanistic system. All silly and remote notions of the justice of an all-powerful God were forcibly squeezed out. The stuffy air and the pounding of my heartbeat made it difficult to freely draw a full breath. My hands were ice cold, and I could not shake the foreboding flutter within my stomach. As I walked into this atheistic darkness, much like bracing for an impending car crash, I thought to myself of how much this was going to hurt.

I was being charged with one count of conspiracy to commit mail fraud, one count of federal perjury, and eight individual counts of mail fraud, which would collectively send me away to prison for at least a decade. The outcome seemed all but certain on that first day, with this jury trial just a meaningless formality. I was also well aware there would be no mercy upon me from Hill and the government for my taking the case this far. I was dead.

As a defendant, it is very difficult to silently sit in the courtroom and listen as witness after witness testifies against you, particularly when they so greatly misrepresent you. The witnesses do not outright lie; they take a small kernel of truth and twist and contort it in such a way as to paint you in the worst possible light. There is really no other alternative but to remain silent and pray that they will have the courage to tell the truth.

This belittling experience was particularly compounded by the absence of certain friends and family during this period. Because of the strong emotion associated with our trial, many stayed away, choosing to avoid a confrontation with their emotions. Although we understood this, it was still disappointing because they could have really supported and helped Laura and me with their presence.

In addition, two of the female staff from the Russians' medical clinic gave in to their fears and chose to testify against me under governmental pressure. Because they were clearly aware of my innocence and unintended involvement in this ordeal, I had never thought they would do this. This is a disappointing betrayal that cuts very deep, particularly when our friendship was largely based on a mutual respect and admiration and seemingly possessed a strength that would have held up against any future obstacle life had to offer. This is why, unless we actually go through circumstances similar to these, when our lives hang in the balance, the pain and hurt of betrayals from false friends cannot be adequately expressed in words. As we desperately try to make eye contact and connect with the people we used to know, the pain and hurt are made unbearable when the words and testimony of the other people are untrue and they are well aware of it. Nonetheless, we have to remember that they chose this path out of weakness in hopes of escaping their fears and surrendered to the basic human instinct of self-preservation.

Fortunately for Laura and me, these episodes were always countered by many other friends and family members who chose to support us with either their presence in the courtroom or their actual courtroom testimony. As I saw these courageous friends and family members shrug off their fear and take the stand in my defense, I always sat a little higher in my chair, forcing myself with great difficulty to hold back a proud smile and a tear. Additionally, my mother attended each day, bringing homemade lunches, making us the envy of the court lunchroom. In times of great difficulty, we shall always be surprised at the individuals around us who choose to rise up and shine, forever remaining in our memory.

As the trial progressed through the first week, something surprising began to happen. This dreaded, dark system of evil which had been seemingly invincible before, now began to lose its intimidating grip of fear on me and show signs of weakness and vulnerability. The devil's greatest weapon against us will always be fear. When we decide to take the fight to him, however, we find that he backs down in cowardice. This is exactly what began to happen.

I was tried with two other individuals because it was a conspiracy case and I was the third and final individual that the government chose to present its case against. The three of us were the last remaining defendants from the original seventeen defendants on our indictment. The other fourteen had quickly pled guilty months before and agreed to testify against us in exchange for lighter sentences. This was the soiled part of our U.S. legal system which I became aware of—a system that routinely pays for the testimony of criminals against potentially innocent defendants and calls it a justice system.

U.S. Attorney Hill took turns with each of us in the order determined by his choosing. After sitting through the cases of the other two defendants before me, I had been witness to their utter destruction against the intelligent, clever, and well-thought-out court strategy employed by the government. I could feel the confidence growing around the crowded government prosecution table. During my case, however, things would go quite differently.

Despite the prosecutors' early sheer dominance, Jim was still very successful during our cross-examinations of the government witnesses called specifically against me. In fact, almost every witness testifying against me for the government ended up admitting upon cross-examination that I had done nothing wrong and had not been involved in any type of criminal conspiracy. In all, we had almost every single witness, event, and fact fall our way as it related to me. To the dismay of the federal prosecutors, these crucial admissions of their own "paid" witnesses even included two Russian organized crime figures called against me.

Light was beginning to shine forth in the darkness at the end of that first week. I recorded a journal entry that night:

8/14/2000 It's been one week into trial and so far so good. "Ah death, where is thy sting?"

I just saw an incredible documentary tonight about an 18 year-old high school football hero, who was paralyzed in an auto accident and the incredible way he handles his hardships. Most strikingly, was a letter written by his Bishop just after the accident:

"I know that some are blaming God for what has happened. You are not. I explained to them that in the pre-existence, we fought for our free agency, which is one of the greatest gifts that our Heavenly Father has given us. It gives us the freedom to act. The flip side of that gift is that it also gives us the freedom to be acted upon. We not only get to enjoy the blessings of a world governed by natural laws but we also get the privilege of being subjected to them. If God were to remove those laws and their governing influence over us, the whole plan of salvation would be disrupted. You have been a high school football

hero. Now you have the chance to be a real hero. Everyone has to deal with some trial by fire. And since yours is presently one of such intense heat, all eyes are upon you to see if your same spirit will prevail. Your example of faith, hope, courage and determination will have a tremendous impact on others."

In his wheelchair, he went on to speak at his high school graduation saying:

"You must play the hand you are dealt. If you can meet with triumph and disaster and treat those two imposters just the same, that is the message. Cherish life. Be happy. It's up to each of us to take control of our own destiny."

After this young man's example I have determined that I have no problems!

As the trial pushed into its third week, the government concluded its case against me and rested. It would now be our turn to tell our story. It was at this time that the unexpected began to unfold within the courtroom. As Laura, I, and a packed courtroom looked on, events began to occur with an increasing frequency as light began to illuminate the empty darkness of this system of atheistic humanism.

Although these events had occurred throughout the entire three weeks of trial, the nature of these miraculous events seemed to be less subtle and much more dramatic as the trial progressed. Now the culmination of our nightmarish ordeal was drawing near. It was almost as if the time had arrived and possessed such significant importance that God no longer saw the need to veil His active hand behind these events. In other words, the gloves came off during this period.

Prepare Thoroughly and Fight Relentlessly

"Behold, I am sending you like sheep in the midst of wolves; so be shrewd as serpents and simple as doves." (Mt 10:16) As Christians, we must learn to thrive amid this apparent paradox from Christ. The life-giving peace and truth of Christ will always be at conflict with the world. To remain mere doves in a world of wolves will do nothing to further God's kingdom on earth. At times, we must stand up and fight for what we believe in, no matter the cost. Sometimes death is preferable to surrender. The Christian paradox simultaneously calls us to fight, to accept persecutions, and to keep our peace and truth.

In eternity, we will learn that the greatest heroes of Christ were His messengers. They were not those who chased after power and prosperity in this life. Their years were spent on higher priorities of eternal consequence. Many of them poured out their hearts for these causes and then bled for them. To be heroes of Christ, we must choose to open the door to the Holy Spirit and have the courage to say, "Speak, your servant is listening. Not my will, but thine be done."

After choosing this path, we'd better get ready. God takes a receptive soul very seriously. Our lives will rapidly change once we've chosen this path. Do it anyway. More than ever, God is in need of messengers within our world. We are being called into a monumental battle of supernatural proportion with human souls at stake. If we fail to answer His call or fail to engage the enemy in battle, souls will be lost.

To become God's messenger, a complete confidence is needed even if what lies ahead is extremely hard. This is a moral leader and something sorely lacking today. Someone who radiates a confident, decided, and strong presence in the face of a difficult mission, with no regard to self, is an incredible inspiration to others. Leaders create worlds that other people want to belong to. Even in our darkest hours, we can be a projection of peace for our families and others. Even if deep down, we possess personal concerns and uncertainties, our impression upon them will remain for a lifetime.

When we choose to answer God's call and become His messengers, we shall always reach points when we must fight for what we believe in. When we courageously fight for truth and justice, we gain assistance as the unexpected begins to happen and a host of miracles spring up around us. It is only after taking the courageous first step in faith against overwhelming odds that we discover that we were never alone; God was simply waiting on us to take our first step in faith. He loves us and greatly respects our free will. We were created to be freely reconciled to Him, not coerced.

We must prepare well before entering the battle, becoming familiar with the tendencies and tactics of our enemy. We must painfully become aware of our own weaknesses, particularly pride, which the enemy shall attempt to exploit. How are we to turn our weakness of pride into a strength? *By ceaselessly placing others first in thought and deed*. This is not always easy, but as we get better at this, we shall see the surprise in the enemy's eyes when his most ferocious assaults harmlessly glance off of us.

We must reside and exist one thought and move ahead of the enemy at all times and have a subsequent response ready to counter him. We should expect to take on minor wounds from the enemy's assaults but remain vigilantly on guard, protecting our most vital organs, when one moment of non-alertness on our part will mean certain death.

We must maintain a heightened focus and concentration, almost without blinking, during the battle. This shall remain until just that instant when we see the first glimpse of retreat and cowardice in the enemy's eyes. In this initial instant of defeat, we call upon and allow our spirit to powerfully rise up within us as we seemingly begin to look down upon our increasingly helpless and shrinking foe.

It is at this moment, as the enemy's chest becomes perfectly exposed for the sharp point of our sword, when the paradox inherent within our Christianity suddenly surfaces once again. As we clutch the enemy's last remaining moments of life within our grasp, our eyes meet his and we recognize and love him as our brother. Upon that recognition, we offer a smile, withdraw our sword and walk away, sparing his life.

Despite the size of the enemy aligned against us, we must always choose to stand up and fight for Christ in our world. This begins when we take the necessary first step in courage and in faith and give God a chance to work His miracles. We must not take the miracle out of God's hands because of our fears. Wage battle courageously. May eternity be our judge!

CHAPTER TEN:

Reaping the Harvest

"For the universe fights on behalf of the just."

Wisdom 16:17

QUITE POSSIBLY, WE HAVE GOTTEN it all wrong regarding the nature of miracles in our lives. Maybe they are not rare at all. Maybe they occur throughout our lives, existing in every minute of every day and, in fact, are the norm of our very existence. We see life as rather non-miraculous because we fail to look deep enough and we mistakenly relegate the miraculous to our narrow criteria of appropriate pomp and grandiosity. This is a shame, because the daily miracles in our lives seldom come gift-wrapped in this type of package.

Such was the case as our trial drew to a close in that third week. We became witness to an avalanche of the miraculous. Apparently, the powerful seeds of earlier bold life choices had now resulted in an abundant harvest. Within this harvest, six incredible events illumined the cold, dark courtroom as God's light overwhelmed the ultimate in worldly human power.

Paralyzing Testimony

The feeling I experienced as I testified in my own defense is difficult to convey in words. On the one hand, I was unbelievably terrified of the experience, feeling a painful isolation in knowing that not a soul on Earth could be with me as I did this. I had a clear and very deep understanding that my words and actions over the next few hours would determine what the rest of my life would be like. This event was compounded as I also knew that the lives of many others would be determined as well—others such as spouses, children, parents, siblings, and many additional individuals who would be touched by the results of this event. The walk from the defendant's table to the testimony stand was the longest walk of my life.

On the other hand, I had never felt so more alive in all my life. I was energized and fueled by the fact I was innocent. When you have such an obvious cause of truth and rightness in your corner and your persecutors have built their foundation on impure deceit and abuse of power, you are left with only one path to travel. You have to aim your car in the direction of truth, push the accelerator to the floor despite the approaching cliff, and put all your faith in the hope of being given wings to softly land in the valley below.

I took the stand as the first of four witnesses called in my defense, which included me and three character witnesses. My entire case was going to hinge on my character and my personal explanation of the facts and events of this case. We had no one else to come to the aid of our defense. My life was in my own hands at that moment.

My testimony on the stand lasted two days and could not have gone any better. In a relaxed and peaceful manner, I was able to clearly and humbly answer every attack leveled against me. For each particular attack, I was able to use words and insight that left the prosecutors no choice but to abandon their line of questioning for that accusation and to move on to a new one. This did not occur once or twice, but rather every time throughout my entire two days of testimony. This eerily resembled the recurrent dream I had experienced over the past four years.

My pretrial preparation with Jim had certainly been adequate but was not the only reason behind the person I had become and who was sitting in court that day. We can never prepare for a cross-examination by a prosecutor who has had a year to prepare the attack upon us. Through God's grace, the testimony must come from deep inside and cannot be rehearsed or memorized, particularly when we possess such clear-cut instances of truth. The majority of answers I gave and the words and phrases I used explaining facts and events during cross-examination were being uttered and discussed for the first time. As in the recurrent dream, my responses were simply a part of me, and I was open and free enough to allow them to flow forth.

I experienced firsthand the promise that Christ made to all of us who choose to believe. He promised His disciples that the Paraclete, or Holy Spirit, will come to us in times such as these, assisting us at the precise moment of need if we remain open. His promises to us are real for those who have faith and believe, and it is truly exciting and life-changing when you experience this firsthand.

The highlight of my testimony came at the end of the first day. To many, this may be one of those small imperceptible daily miracles that are so easy to take for granted. For those with eyes to see and ears to hear, however, this was truly the Paraclete in action.

The courtroom was packed, with not an open seat to be found. Jim was concluding his direct examination of me and was going to end the day after my explanation of the day of my arrest. Throughout my testimony up until that point, Hill and his prosecutors strongly objected repeatedly to every question my attorney asked and every answer I gave that appeared to disadvantage their prosecution. This greatly interrupted our momentum and our ability to tell our side of the story and was extremely frustrating.

In addition, Agent Hennessey and Agent Stone continued to sit at the prosecutor's table in full view of the courtroom. With coordinated gestures and facial expressions, they would react to each of Jim's questions and my answers in an attempt to display to the jury the importance or irrelevance of each point. This had taken place throughout the trial, but during my testimony, it seemed to intensify, as if they too realized that the entire trial's outcome hinged on my few hours of testimony.

I had just explained how the government had arrested me at my home with five-year-old Madison present to witness it. The point was also made regarding the common practice of allowing non-threatening white collar defendants to voluntarily surrender in most other cases. As I finished, I was surprised to not be abruptly stopped by Hill's objections, as had been his repeated practice throughout my testimony.

Surprisingly, Jim was permitted to continue through this sudden silence on the part of the government. "Dr. Norman, what else happened on that day?"

After waiting for the objection that never came, I responded by pointing to Agent Stone as he sat smugly in front of me at the prosecutor's table. "I opened the door, and *this* FBI agent right here forced me face first into the wall and handcuffed me!"

As I pointed out the agent for the jury to see, I witnessed stunned silence from the previously objecting prosecutor's table. They were motionless and speechless as the specifics of my arrest were no longer concealed and now clearly out in the open for the courtroom to see. It was as if they had become so caught up in the story themselves that they had become spectators along with the rest of the packed court-room.

Everything changed after that moment. The jury became notice-ably shaken, upset, and angry as their attention turned toward the federal agents, who were slowly shrinking into their chairs. The packed courtroom suddenly erupted into a roar. I will always remem-ber the looks on the faces of the court spectators as one of shock, sym-pathy, and then anger all in one instant.

I remember seeing the look on Jim's face. Despite his more than twenty-five years of courtroom experience and his full awareness of the specifics of my arrest, he seemed to be suddenly struck again by the injustice of this entire ordeal. In that one instant, Jim was reminded once again of the reason for all of the hours of preparation for this case and the reason for becoming an attorney in the first place many years ago.

The miracle in this instant was witnessed by anyone who looked over at the prosecutor's table, where a once overconfident Hill was now looking increasingly humble. This damaging fact that the gov-ernment desperately wanted to conceal was now out in the open where all could see. During my answer, it was almost as if an invisi-ble force had been holding the government team in their chairs, pre-venting them from standing up to object. The truth refused to be bottled up any longer.

As I spoke, the prosecutors had been sitting on the edge of their chairs, captivated by the story and seemingly having forgotten all prosecutorial responsibilities. Upon seeing the growing chaos over-taking his courtroom, it was the judge who finally halted the pro-ceedings. He silenced the courtroom with his gavel and called all attorneys up to his bench in an attempt to regain order.

The previously stoic federal judge now had the look of surprised disappointment for his government colleagues—almost the look of a helpless father who could not step in to help his sons, able only to urge them on silently to recover from their misstep. During the brief few minutes of the judge's private conference, I could overhear him ask the prosecution for their explanation of what was happening. "Counsel, why are you allowing this proceeding to get out of hand?" he questioned.

As I remained seated on the stand directly in front of the prose-cutor's table, I witnessed the two once proud and arrogant federal agents who remained seated at the table. For the first time, the sinis-ter smirk of Agent Hennessey and the arrogant posturing of Agent

Stone were long since gone. Demoralized and very uncomfortable, the agents refused to make any type of further eye contact with the nearby jury or myself.

Angels on the Freeway

The very next day, on the morning of my second day of testimony, another incredible occurrence took place during my testimony on the stand. This occurrence, however, involved Laura. It occurred before the court session began for that day.

Laura took Madison to school in our car while I went to the downtown federal courthouse on the bus that morning. The plan was for us to all ride home together that evening after the long day in court. This was a very important day in court, as I was going to resume my testimony on the stand after the incredible fireworks of the day before. As I was called up to the stand to resume my testimony, I was very surprised to still see no sign of Laura.

My testimony on the second day picked up right where it had left off. I continued to be guided with just the right words, responses, and explanations needed for each accusation. The endless free-flowing nature of this guidance, as well as the wonderful feeling of aliveness, continued throughout the remainder of this cruel inquisition. I remember being somewhat happy and relieved to see Laura finally enter the courtroom thirty minutes into the proceedings and take her familiar seat in the right first-row gallery. It was not until later that evening that I learned the full extent for the reason of her late arrival and the small miracle she had experienced.

Laura had just taken Madison to school that morning and was driving downtown to the courthouse on the freeway. As she approached downtown, she prepared to enter a high one-lane southbound bridge that would loop her around into the downtown area. Just a few seconds before arriving at the bridge, she saw a huge 2'x3' block of concrete break loose from a cement truck immediately in front of her! Because it was directly in her lane and she was surrounded by morning rush hour traffic, she was too close to avoid the inevitable impact. She slammed head-on into the concrete block at full freeway speed. With a sound that can be likened only to an explosion, the concrete block ripped through the undercarriage of her car and exploded all four tires.

Somehow, Laura was able to maintain control of the car and maneuver it to the shoulder and guardrail of the freeway. Amazingly enough, she was uninjured, despite her jangled nerves and the utter destruction of her car. Looking back later, she recalled a very eerie occurrence during this incident.

Before the impact, in the midst of morning rush hour traffic, she had been traveling on a busy downtown freeway with cars all around her. At the time of impact, however, all the cars had seemed to disappear. There was nobody around her! In typical rush hour traffic in downtown Dallas, she certainly should have been rear-ended after her impact and possibly propelled into other cars or into the guardrail. Despite her post-accident shock, she was already thinking, *This was typical morning rush hour traffic just a few seconds ago!*

Nonetheless, despite this miracle, she sat entrapped helplessly on the shoulder of the freeway within her destroyed car and unable to get to the courthouse on this crucial day of trial. She could only break down and cry. In between her sobs, she prayed and asked God for help. She remembers asking for an angel.

No sooner had this plea come off her lips than she was startled by a loud knocking on her car window. Laura opened her eyes and looked up to find the friendly face of an elderly female motorist who had witnessed everything and stopped to help. Still crying as she rolled down her window, Laura was even more shaken by the initial words of this gentle, friendly stranger. "Consider me your angel today," the stranger said.

The motorist was a very friendly and extremely gentle elderly woman simultaneously conveying a deep inner strength. This instantly calmed Laura's anxiety and brought her out of her state of shock. This was when Laura's thoughts returned to our court trial and the urgency of the second day of my testimony. "I have to get to the courthouse. My husband is on trial," Laura told the woman, having no further concern about her car.

She didn't have to explain any further; it was as if the sweet, gentle old woman already knew everything. She drove Laura to the front door of the courthouse. Laura got out and turned to thank the woman. "Thank you very much. You *are* my angel today!" she said.

"You are surrounded by angels, sweetie, not just today. Now go. Be with your husband," the friendly woman said as she gave Laura a warm smile.

In her morning of chaos and near tragedy, Laura felt a strong sense of peace as the woman drove away.

The Disappearing Voice

This event during trial is one of my favorites as well as a favorite of my family simply because it was so incredible. It occurred as we neared the end of the trial and it came time for Jim to call upon our witnesses to testify. It had always been planned that I would take the stand and that would be our primary means of defense; however, we were unsure about who to call as additional supportive character witnesses to add to my case. The list of possibilities had to include strong individuals who could face intense cross-examination with good communication skills, possess good character, and add credibility to my defense. It was truly a difficult decision as we weighed the advantages and disadvantages of calling each one as a witness.

One of the witnesses Jim really felt we should call was my father. He wanted to show the jury what kind of close, strong, supportive family I came from and bring out my father's trademark honesty and integrity. Ordinarily, I would have thought this was a good idea, but at this time I disagreed and debated with Jim many times on this subject.

My father was a hardworking man who struggled to make a life for his family. Very little came easily to him. He was a man of his word and had unquestionable loyalty toward all who knew him. Taking shortcuts in life was not part of his makeup. After he had gone to work at age seventeen, the next four decades were filled with family sacrifice and a forgoing of his own personal dreams. Now, about to lose a son, the unfairness and injustice of our ordeal had to be unbearable for him.

The incredibly stressful nature of this entire ordeal left my father in a difficult state. He seemed to be incapable of grasping the intricate details of the case, and the momentous number of facts all seemed to run together in his mind. He had difficulty remembering the dates, people, and important events that were crucial in gaining an understanding of this case. I did not think it was wise to put him on the stand. Despite my protests, Jim was ultimately successful in convincing me that my father would greatly benefit our case as a witness. For this reason, we were all set to call him to the stand for his testimony during the final week of the trial.

As the day finally arrived for us to call our witnesses, they were all ready except one. That morning when my father awoke, he discovered that he could not speak. I am certainly aware that everybody comes down with a case of hoarseness or laryngitis every now and then. This was not one of those cases, however. My father had absolutely no voice! There was no conceivable explanation for this condition, such as a cold, an allergy, or any previous condition. He later told us this had never occurred to him in his life and he had no explanation whatsoever.

Needless to say, we were forced that day to call on some alternate witnesses who filled in quite well and assisted my defense greatly. My father had to simply sit and watch the proceedings that day as his sudden condition of muteness continued. As the day ended and Jim rested our case, another incredible event occurred. When our family went to dinner that evening, all sitting around the table, we were amazed to witness my father's voice return just as quickly as it had been lost. You be the judge.

Divine Light

The following occurrence will surely be discounted in the minds of most people who hear of it. It can easily be explained away as simply someone's failure to change out a courtroom light bulb in a timely manner. To me and many other individuals who were there to witness it, however, this event became a symbol of something much more: a reassuring sign to me of God's will and a source of strength and peace.

My case was a conspiracy trial, and, as such, multiple defendants were being tried at once—three in my case. The defendants were situated on the left side of the courtroom, and the government prosecutors were on the right. Each of the three defendants and their attorneys were given their own table and placed in a location and order chosen by the prosecution according to the order in which we would be tried. My attorneys and I found ourselves at the third and final table on the far left of the courtroom, directly across the room from the jury. The federal prosecutors had chosen to prosecute our case last after the other two defendants' cases.

We had four people at our table, including myself; Jim; Gina, a female attorney assisting us; and Mandi, an invaluable female legal assistant who sat behind us to quickly retrieve documents and files. Gina and Mandi provided the trial its only female legal presence in the male-dominated courtroom.

Much like family, the four of us sat huddled around the large dark-brown legal table for the entire three-week trial. We worked very well together, and our teamwork was evident, with each of us knowing our particular job responsibilities. During difficult periods of the trial, I would periodically alternate glances between my great team of friends and a tiny golden locket that I kept on the table in front of me. This locket contained a picture of Madison and my nephew Tanner. These glances strengthened me and reminded me of why I was fighting.

The four of us actually looked as if a courtroom defendants' table was the last place on Earth at which we belonged. Jim's tall, thin, clean-cut gentlemanly appearance and his relaxed and friendly Southern drawl instantly put anyone at ease and gave reason to trust him. Gina and Mandi's appearance instantly struck up feelings of honesty, sincerity, and sweetness, softening up the cold, callous, impersonal male-dominated courtroom.

Throughout these weeks, I periodically felt the puzzled stares aimed in my direction from the jury, the court reporter, the other defendants' attorneys, various gallery spectators, and even the judge. I felt like they all had the same question: *What could that guy have possibly done wrong to be in a place like this?* And this was all before we uttered our first words in defense, as we sat quietly awaiting the cases against the other defendants to conclude. Such was our appearance at that third and final defendants' table, sitting alone at the far left of the courtroom during the trial.

Our appearance to those in the courtroom, however, seemed to become even more magnified through no act of our own. It appeared that an overhead florescent light directly over our table would periodically surge, intensifying its light, shining its brightness down upon us. It would only occur once or twice a day throughout the trial, but it seemed to occur at the most opportune moments. The effect of this was very noticeable to all those present, who would shift their glances toward us each time it occurred.

This florescent light, with its periodic illumination of the four of us at our table, offered a brief but radiant brightness within the dull and drab courtroom. In this otherwise properly functioning light, a nondisruptive sound was also audible only to us during surges, and it was never mentioned by courtroom personnel as something that required repair. These occurrences reached their apex at the end of the trial during Jim's closing argument.

As Jim took the courtroom through the cruel account of our six-year nightmare, we were all taken on an emotional roller coaster that seemed to build in intensity as he neared his argument's conclusion. Precisely at the perfect time and at the height of this intensity, as he concluded to a now tearful courtroom, the florescent light delivered its biggest surge yet. As if the light were delivering a grand finale, our table was illumined in whiteness, causing the courtroom to suddenly pause and look over. As jury, judge, court reporter, and gallery looked over at us, my mother, seated in the gallery, began to cry at this dramatic but obvious sign from above.

A Day of Grace Overflowing

The courtroom, particularly the criminal courtroom, is a very cold and impersonal place. I found it to contain a certain emptiness, devoid of all emotion, that strikes you the moment you walk in. For a majority of the time, our criminal courtrooms are home to the very worst of our society day in and day out. Much like the medical staff at an E.R. trauma center, courtroom employees must eventually learn to keep their emotions at a distance and gradually become desensitized to the wide range of daily events within their courtroom. So it is with reason of necessity that the courtroom becomes such a cold and impersonal place, as reflected through its human elements such as judges, prosecutors, bailiffs, court reporters, and even jurors in many circumstances.

This is why this occurrence is very special to me. Although it may not be classified as a miracle, the effect of my case upon the individuals within the courtroom was no ordinary occurrence. They broke out of this cold structure of humanism and became genuine and authentic human beings again, with a show of emotion that could not be contained despite their best efforts.

It seemed to have started one year earlier, at my arraignment hearing, where I made my first appearance before the judge in my case. My *un-criminal-like* nature began to strike people as not congruent with the government's accusations against me. My arraignment hearing and the judge's reaction to me were simply the start of a great impact my case would exact on his courtroom. The actual trial lasted three weeks and contained many other instances such as this. Even before I had spoken my first word of testimony, it seemed I had already been firmly positioned in the perception of everybody except the government prosecutors as they all wondered, *What could this person have possibly done to be here?*

This perception was conveyed to me in many ways. At times, it was obvious through a verbal exchange, but others were more subtle, through facial expressions, eye contact, and periodic small extensions of respect. With the exception of Hill, Agent Hennessey, and Agent Stone, who steadfastly refused to let any aspect of truth impact their version of events, this became my experience with every other individual involved with my case within that courtroom. Moreover, during Jim's closing argument, going even beyond the fluorescent light episode, the full emotional impact of my case on each of these individuals reached its pinnacle. For those individuals present that day, all were left with an experience that will not soon be forgotten.

Although we had only a brief fifty-two minutes, Jim was some-how successful in telling the courtroom the entire story of our ordeal within his closing argument. In true Atticus Finch style, Jim used his affable Southern personality to methodically extricate the truth from the weakening grip of those who were deceptively suppressing it. With passion and a deep thundering and resounding voice, he took the courtroom through the past six years of our life and made every-one feel as if they had experienced those years personally. The entire courtroom finally learned of all the cruel pain, anguish, paralyzing fear, and anxiety that had smothered the lives of Laura, Madison, and me.

The courtroom was again packed completely full, with many spectators standing in the back. The word had gotten out, and the trial had begun to garner publicity. Media were in attendance, as were many attorneys who had taken the day off to sit in on the pro-ceedings. Jim was like an old war general who returned to fight one last battle. In the legal community, he was a living legend, particu-larly among the younger attorneys. On that day, Jim was a master, and everybody had come to sit at his feet and watch him work.

Despite Jim's nearly twenty-five years of practice and countless trials, this was different. After I spoke with his friends and colleagues much later, they told me they had never seen him like this before. His passionate and heart-wrenching closing argument would be talked about in the legal community for months afterward. His emotionally charged argument, his obvious personal attachment to my case, his belief in my innocence, and his anger at the system's corruptness far transcended those in any trial argument he had delivered in the past. On that day, he could just as well have been defending his own son.

This became more than just another day in court for all of us. Our story, as related through Jim, seemed to impact others in a very powerful way. Our bold life choices had opened this door, but I was now witnessing God's grace overflowing with nothing of my doing. Regardless of who they were or what duties they performed in that courtroom that day, everyone saw this fact become obvious. God was leading us all to become different people than we had been when the day had begun.

The first person greatly affected by these emotions was me. As I sat there and listened to our six-year ordeal, I could not hold back any longer. Simultaneously, I felt anger about what had been done to us, relief that our story was finally being told to people who had the power to help, and pride that I had chosen to fight this. I was now witnessing the materialization of the reward for taking this leap of faith and courage. I cried and cried, and the table at which I sat soon overflowed with wadded-up Kleenex after nearly an hour of tears.

The jury was the source of the next noticeable exhibition of emotion. Tears began to fill their eyes as they sat in stunned silence and experienced the same emotions as I. Their anger at the corruptness of the system became palpably apparent as they again heard how Agent Hennessey had tailored my false confession and falsified federal documents. As the jurors glanced toward the federal prosecutors and the two federal agents, their facial expressions turned to disgust. I could read the jury's subconscious body language as they folded their arms and leaned back within their chairs to place themselves as far away from the government as they could get.

I next noticed the female court reporter, who was seated in front of the judge and had been busily typing for the past three weeks of the trial. During this emotional closing argument, I saw her with tears running down her cheeks despite her many years of hearing trial testimony. With difficulty, she had to wipe her tears away quickly to keep up with her typewritten account of the proceeding.

My attention then turned to Mr. Payne, the six-foot-five African-American courtroom bailiff. To me, his powerful presence made him seem seven-foot-five. Throughout the three weeks of trial, he had remained stoic and unmoved by the proceedings, although always professional, courteous, and polite to all. During the closing argument, however, I perceived a look of disgust and resentment on his face as he glanced toward the all-white federal prosecutor's table and his governmental employers. I remember feeling his smile underneath his stoic exterior as he witnessed justice being served. In effect, it felt like we were now on the same team as we buried our common persecutors of oppression and prejudice, letting justice flow down as waters, and righteousness like a mighty stream. (Amos 5:24)

Then my glance turned to the federal judge, who possessed the job of dispensing justice and righting the wrongs as he saw fit. Although he was stoic and emotionless, it was obvious that, as a representative of his federal colleagues, he desired no further association with them. The ship was going down, and he wanted off. His focus was on regaining his credibility and the control of his courtroom. His governmental agents had been exposed as corrupt, deceitful, and misleading human beings and had placed him in quite a predicament.

With mountainous examples of manufactured evidence, doctored reports, coerced testimony, and a false confession, the judge, I believe was truly thankful that my trial was not greatly publicized by the media. If it had been, he would have been roasted by the community to reprimand the agents' conduct. Rather, this case would be allowed to silently fade away and die with only a minimal amount of press coverage.

Gathering from the judge's words and actions for the remainder of my trial, it was obvious he no longer looked at me as a defendant. The judge began to treat me as a victim of his federal prosecutors and agents, whom he repulsively began to distance himself from. This case, however, along with his agents' conduct, would undoubtedly inhabit a permanent place within his mind in any future proceedings.

This distance would continue despite the still prideful efforts of Hill to salvage the case. In a desperate attempt to connect with the jury on a human level, the government took a shot in the dark that would never be found in any legal textbooks. In his trademark manner of nonchalant disinterest, but still unable to shake his underlying arrogance, Hill stood at the podium and left the jury with a strange final charge. "Look, I know Dr. Norman is probably a nice person. We have seen in this trial that he comes from a good family. But you have seen the evidence against him. It comes down to this...if you think the government was corrupt and lied, go ahead and acquit this man!" he said as he turned and pointed back toward me.

With that, he threw up his arms in resignation, reclaimed his seat, and avoided any further eye contact with the jury. For a brief instant, I saw that this was all one big game for the federal agents and prosecutors. At the end of the day, they would go home and not give a second thought to the lives affected by their actions. My family and I were absolutely inconsequential in the face of their agenda in what had been merely a six-year game. A game that was quickly drawing to a close.

Goliath Finally Falls

This all-around display of emotion in the previously cold and impersonal courtroom culminated on that final day. As the jury returned with their verdict, I sensed twelve people with a mission as they were ushered in to take their seats. One juror in particular made the strongest impression on Laura and me. She was a friendly, tall, heavyset African-American woman who radiated a powerful strength from the juror box. She sat directly in the center of the juror box, and her strength seemingly guided and led the other jurors. Throughout the trial, her periodic glances and expressions toward the prosecution table were evident and I saw her disdain for the corrupt, power-hungry federal prosecutors.

As the twelve jurors took their seats, it was this particular juror who searched out Laura's face in the first-row gallery. Upon finding Laura, the woman gave her a reassuring smile and wink, causing Laura to break out into joyous tears. Laura actually knew of the verdict a full five minutes before I would hear it!

"Have you, the jury, reached a verdict?" the judge asked.

"We have, Your Honor," spoke the jury foreman, handing over the verdict sheet.

"In that case, will the defendant please rise."

As I stood up to await the pronouncement upon my life and my family's life, the moment seemed to stretch into an eternity. The air in the packed courtroom was thick with tension; we could hear a pin drop. Many within the local legal community were still on hand in the gallery, as news of this case through news reports and word-of-mouth gossip continued to spread.

I held my breath and clenched my fists so hard that my fingernails dug into my palms. All of life ceased for these moments as the people, activities, and sounds all became muted. I was in an air-tight tunnel of silence, with all my focus on the judge's voice and his reading of the jury's verdict sheet.

"In the case of the United States versus Michael Norman..."
NOT GUILTY.

We had done the impossible: fully acquitted on all nine counts, with the tenth count being already dismissed! I looked at Laura in her first-row gallery seat and defiantly pumped my fist in the air at her. Looking at Laura, I could see at that moment all the pain she had been forced to endure over these six years and the emotional toll it had taken on her. Our teary eyes were fixed on each other for what seemed like forever.

As the jury returned our lives back to us, I think I was in shock and really did not feel anything. There would be plenty of time in the months and years ahead to allow all of this to sink in. For the moment, I simply remained in a state of numb exhilaration.

After the verdict was announced, Laura and I left the courtroom and met the jurors, who were also leaving. They hugged us and told us how sorry they were for what was done. "We could feel the prayers coming from you guys. It was unanimous. We were not going to let them get good Christian people," they told us, smiling.

I thanked each of the jurors and apologized for imposing on their lives over these past three weeks.

"We were glad to be here and stop all of this. Now, go home to your family and start enjoying life again!"

We did not see any jury members that day—only twelve angels who came into our lives for those three weeks.

As we made our way out of the upstairs courtroom corridor, I heard a deep voice booming behind me, trying to get my attention. It was Mr. Payne, the towering courtroom bailiff. "Congratulations, Dr. Norman," he said, shaking my hand.

As my hand disappeared within his massive handshake, the respectful gleam in his eye and the smile on his face finally betrayed the professional stoicism he was forced to keep in the courtroom. At that moment, we both realized that we are very much alike and stand for the same principles. He was obviously moved after seeing somebody finally stand up and fight against the oppressive system that all too often daily tramples upon those principles.

As Laura and I finally made it down to the lobby, we ran into another courtroom participant. As we awaited family members before leaving the lobby, we were approached by Dana, the court reporter for our trial. Smiling and very excited, she told me, "Dr. Norman, I am really glad you won! I have never cried at a trial before and I wanted you to win. I am sorry for everything that happened to you guys."

Laura and I thanked her very much and wished her well. As we prepared to leave the courthouse, we had no way of knowing one more big surprise awaited.

As Laura briefly went back upstairs to retrieve family members, my father and I remained in the massive lobby of the federal courthouse, which was quickly emptying on that late Friday afternoon. Very soon, we found ourselves all alone. Out of the corner of my eye, I noticed a figure approaching us from the other end of the lobby. As I turned to greet this fast-approaching stranger, I instantly recognized him.

With a look of sincerity that I had not before seen in him, Agent Hennessey extended his hand for a handshake. With a noticeable absence of his sinister smirk, the lead agent of this case and the person primarily responsible for my indictment and prosecution spoke first. "Dr. Norman, congratulations. I am sorry that all this happened. I hope in the future we can meet under better circumstances."

As my father looked on, wondering how I would react, I could only summon one response. "Thank you," I said simply as we shook hands.

With that, Agent Hennessey walked off, leaving us alone again in the lobby.

Many people have told me they probably would not have been so nice to the arch-nemesis of our ordeal. After all, it had been exposed in trial that his investigation of me included doctored reports, known false testimony, and a false confession. Our six-year ordeal, including federal indictment, a raid on our home, arrest and federal prosecution, was largely based on the deceitful investigative work of this one individual. However, I can answer only with the truth.

At that moment and continuing to this day, I cannot muster an ounce of ill will toward this agent even if I try. Beginning at that point, despite the difficulties, I was aware of all the blessings that had already come into our lives as a result. Without him and his actions, these blessings could not have occurred.

* * *

My trial began as a willful surrender to the inevitable, being crushed by the ultimate in worldly power and humanism. I fully accepted this and was prepared to suffer the painful consequences which lay ahead if it was God's will. After three long weeks in that cold, dark, and impersonal courthouse, however, we found it to actually contain much bright light in the end.

My trial introduced me to many of these bright lights in the form of loving and caring ordinary people who chose to rise up and shine from beneath the shadows of a few corrupt and very powerful individuals. I learned, despite the well-orchestrated and concerted efforts of evil, that light, when we choose it and stand up for it, shall always overwhelm the darkness. As one person stands up for light, others are encouraged to stand up and join the battle.

As Laura and I drove home that day, we experienced the most incredible feeling of elation imaginable. I am certain that winning a Super Bowl would not even come close to this. We had gotten our lives back. We had been under such a dark, foreboding cloud of pressure and stress for so long, and now it was suddenly lifted. We rejoined Madison at home and embraced in the longest group hug ever.

God's greatest gift to us, the power of choice, had unexpectedly opened an extraordinary door for us. It led to a completely new world. This new world was one God had desired for us all along but first needed our cooperation for. Little did we know that the best was yet to come. Before receiving His abundant gifts, however, Laura and I would have to adjust to living in this new world and would have to experience some temporary growing pains.

Bet the Farm on Him

It has been wisely said that death is victorious in those who cling to life. This is certainly true, but it should also be stressed that this is a *slow* death. Nowhere has this been more evident than in the modern developed world in which we live. Risk, in all its forms, has become a bad word. We are constantly encouraged to seek out the rational and responsible ideals of security, safety and comfort in all areas of life. This appeals to our basic instincts of fear and self-preservation, and over time, we are lulled into a timid sleep of complacency that consumes the best years of our lives. Instead of heights of achievement, we become a shadow of the people we could have become. Life becomes a spectator sport and we make our choice by making no choice.

Life holds no security. Risk is the reality. It is risky to change, grow, love, and reach out to others. We risk failure, rejection, or losing those we love. God even took a risk by creating us and giving us the power of choice. His earthly ministry was one of daily risk, and His message incessantly urges us to put ourselves on the line. God's kingdom will never be ushered in without risk.

Allow the irony to seep in. Life becomes most precious to us after we have found a reason for which we would give it up. What would we give our lives for? Money? Fame? Power? At life's conclusion, these empty ideals abandon us for other, more promising prospects. There is only one sure bet.

Give your days to the One who can create all out of nothingness. When we choose Him, we cannot lose. Even if we give our entire lives and meet with seeming failure in the eyes of the world, we still win in the end.

How can we accomplish this? We have a supernatural nature and are worthy of supernatural blessings. To receive our rightful supernatural blessings, we must first sow supernatural seeds. A supernatural seed is no less than the unconditional surrender of our *entire* lives, in season and out of season.

The blessings of God await us in every second of every day. It's up to us. We merely have to accept the risk, step up, and choose. God is never limited in the size of His miracles for us. All limitations reside within us. The bolder our choices for Him, the more dramatic the harvest. The bigger the bet for Him, the greater the payout. As the seeds of our wise choices are deeply planted in a rich and nutritious soil, God will faithfully send a bountiful harvest in His time.

Once it is started, always remember that the harvest will continue to return abundantly each season. Accept His gifts and thank Him by continued rededication. His future for us keeps expanding if we allow it. Do not let current blessings get in the way of future blessings.

After our unconditional choices, God will first call us to serve those right under our noses: our families, blood relation or not. No success can ever compensate for a failure to our spouses, children, parents, siblings, friends, and neighbors. He calls us to die for them. This is not easy, but there is no greater work in all of our world. If we succeed in this task, our reward will be unimaginable.

God has placed us and called us to spiritually lead our families for a reason. This is His plan to populate Heaven. Stand up and fight for them, holding together what the world would desperately like to destroy. It is a battle we must win.

Familial love is a risk. We take the chance of being rejected, hurt, and used by some who are quite unlovable. We also risk losing those we have deeply entrusted our hearts to. Risk it anyway. Always risk on the side of love. God can turn the unlovable into the lovable overnight. And for those whom we have lost, God has defeated death and shall reunite us all very soon.

Beware of voices calling you away from family. Our God is a God of unity. God's voice is never the one that calls us away from family. When Christ called Peter, Peter's family was included also. Peter's entire family received the benefit of Christ's ministry. (Mt 8:14–15)

It is far too late to be indecisive at this point. The wounds of humanity are too great and are getting worse. To heal these wounds, God needs to use us now. It will take a supernatural seed. Often, it will include people in our very own families. There will always be risk. Embrace it and bet the farm on He who created the universe. He is a sure thing. When we do, we win here and in Heaven.

CHAPTER ELEVEN:

The Uneasy Calm

"He said not: thou shalt not be troubled—thou shalt not be tempted—thou shalt not be distressed. But He said: thou shalt not be overcome."

Blessed Julian of Norwich

IN HOLLYWOOD, AS WELL AS in many novels on the *New York Times* bestseller list, our story would have ended happily and triumphantly at the conclusion of our court vindication. Real life is always quite different, however. The most incredible blessings will always be accompanied by struggles and difficulties. When we follow the will of God and trust Him with our futures, there will be a price to pay. The journey of faith is far from a triumphal march to victory. It is a daily struggle, mixed with periods of progress and falling back.

In Matthew's gospel account, a violent storm was tossing and swamping the boat containing Jesus and His disciples. Upon waking and rebuking the winds and sea, Jesus restored a great calm while His disciples watched in amazement. In this serene and peaceful calm that followed the violent storm, however, the first thing Jesus and His disciples encountered next on the shore were the demons of Satan. This was our family's experience also.

As the calm sets in after a traumatic event, we become strangers in a strange land. The terrain of God's new world is foreign to us. We have outgrown our old spaces and feel as though we no longer fit in anywhere. The demons that follow the calm of the storm make their presence known here.

The calm of the storm is a time of great uncertainty, confusion, and a somewhat mournful state of sentimental longing for our comfortable pre-trauma routines and existences. Everything is reassessed during this time, from ideals to vocations, careers, priorities, and relationships. In this state, we frequently meet with fatigue, depression, lack of motivation, apathy, and, many times, stress-related health problems.

Upon surrendering to God's will and accepting the inevitability of going away to prison for all those years, Laura and I were totally unprepared for what ultimately happened. Actually winning our court case against the mighty U.S. government had been beyond our most distant expectations. I had made peace with putting to death my old life and had prepared my family for this result as well. Upon returning to our old life, we had no idea of where to begin or how to resume.

Financially speaking, we were devastated. We quickly learned that despite our innocence and victory, there is very limited opportunity for individuals wrongly caught up in these scenarios to recover legal fees from the government. We explored a vague law that provides an exonerated federal defendant the opportunity to file a claim against the federal government to recover legal expenses. This option requires significantly more legal fees to be paid, is rarely ever granted, and could take years to resolve. Laura and I were in no position to fund this battle, and we chose to end the ordeal, walk away, and begin to rebuild our lives.

At the onset of the ordeal, our meager financial assets had been quickly liquidated to pay the massive legal fees. IRAs, retirement accounts, 401k accounts, and any household possessions of value (except Laura's wedding ring) evaporated overnight. We had remortgaged our home and handed the home equity check directly over to the legal system. The financial crush of being buried alive by the U.S. legal system is not easily overcome. Today, several years later, Laura and I continue to dig our way out of this pit with frustratingly slow progress.

Although Laura and I somehow managed to save our home throughout the ordeal, we sold it soon after my acquittal for some much-needed cash. This would be the start of four moves over the next three years. The three of us initially took up residence for many months in a bedroom within my parents' home. Surprisingly, over time, something special began to happen to us amid our utter financial ruin.

As a family, we all learned to travel lightly with regard to material possessions. Our years of accumulated stuff were packed away in boxes in a storage facility. We soon discovered that we really did not miss it. We focused instead on being together through a host of board games, backyard soccer matches, and endless conversations at the family dinner table. Through the intensity of our ordeal and the aftermath, the priorities of life continued to become strongly ingrained within us. Our entire family instinctively banded together as a clan against the onslaught. We learned that if we have each other, nothing else matters.

The emotional toll taken upon our family was also extremely heavy, particularly with Madison, who endured much of this trauma subconsciously because of her young age. Shortly after my acquittal, as we were playing one day at home, we gained a glimpse into some of the subconscious anger and anxiety she felt, which can be instilled into any traumatized child. Completely out of character, six-year-old Madison just started punching and hitting me repeatedly. As my arms and back took the punishment, Laura and I let her finish. Thankfully, as the months passed, the emotional toll upon Madison diminished, including her anxiety over the ringing of our doorbell.

Stress is a silent killer that affects all of us. As the normal defenses of the body break down under the continuous traumatic assault, the body's fight-or-flight mechanism becomes exhausted. This renders individuals defenseless to a myriad of health issues.

Throughout our ordeal, the extreme stress caused internal damage to our bodies. It felt as if we had aged decades over those six years. Laura required surgery for internal complications due to stress. In addition, our threshold, or capacity to handle future stress, was severely impaired. In essence, previously minor obstacles now became great mountains to climb. For Laura and me, this period of our lives felt as if we were walking with cement in our shoes no matter what we did.

Shortly after the acquittal, I began to experience a fairly common phase of emotional healing. We felt God had preserved our lives for great and noble causes, and we were plagued with guilt for not immediately repaying His favor with supernatural human efforts. I experienced this period as a frenzied time of championing all types of life changes. I organized a new political group, led social causes, nearly sold my practice and moved our family, and even contemplated entering law school. All of these quickly ran their course and simply left me exhausted.

I learned that this is a period when we need consistent wise counsel. I began to meet with Father John again and learned of the wisdom of avoiding major life decisions in the immediate aftermath of suffering or major trauma.

"Be patient. These are not the voices of the Holy Spirit," Father John would gently counsel, reigning me back in.

As I followed this advice and avoided the temptations of the demons, this temporary, frenzied state gradually ran its course. I was traumatized, wounded, and on the rebound, and my life choices were all wrong for me at this time. Fortunately, I avoided a compounded tragedy brought on by rash decisions, poor judgment, and heightened emotion. As this frenzied state subsides, we are able to slowly grow and assimilate into our larger realm of existence and God's new life plan. It is almost as if we are breaking in a new pair of shoes.

I experienced another particularly trying cross in the aftermath of our ordeal that I really did not understand for several years. I have since learned this is a very common experience among those who have endured long periods of trauma, suffering, or extreme stress. Although Laura was not as afflicted as I was, this experience was a period of deep depression that affected both of us. With remnants continuing to this day, this posed a foe almost tougher to beat than the U.S. government.

During our ordeal, despite the pain of suffering and the extreme feelings of uncertainty, fear, and anxiety, Laura and I never felt closer to God than we had during that time. We both found that only the human experience and gift of suffering has the ability to bring us this close to God. Although painful, it was truly the way God chose to unite with us.

Throughout our ordeal, it seemed as though in the times of our greatest pain, hopelessness, and anxiety, Laura and I were given comparable consolations of peace and serenity. These feelings of peace and serenity would frequently come from the most ordinary and common places such as book passages, lines from a movie, or scenes from nature. They would be sufficient enough for us to overpower the pain and face another day.

Many times, I felt so close to God that I could hear His words and know His thoughts. In what should have been the worst of times, I was given a blessed gift of seeing behind the veil and experiencing brief periods of consolation that human words cannot describe. These were extremely brief encounters of wonderful intimacy with God; nonetheless, they were enough to send one to the ends of the Earth to experience again.

Soon after the acquittal, however, Laura and I felt ourselves moving away from this warm embrace. Although we experienced this differently, both of us felt as if we were slowly moving outside into the dark, cold night. We desperately tried to get back inside but could not, despite our best attempts. This was very painful and began to exhibit itself as a deepening depression in each of us. I could no longer hear Him speak to us as He once had or know His will for us as clearly as I once had known.

This experience was compounded by the constant feeling of letting God down after He had done so much for us. I felt like He had spared our lives for a reason by granting us an unimaginable feat and deliverance from our ordeal. In His doing so, I felt like I was meant to do equally great things for Him in return. This led to my hyperactive frenzied state of activity. As I found myself mired in weakness, fatigue, and uncertainty because of this dark cloud of depression, God's silence was extremely painful. After having stayed strong for so long, I was ashamed of my current lack of strength. I increasingly faced a world that I could no longer function in.

My prayer life during this period changed dramatically. I would pray hard and often, desperately trying to reconnect like I had before, asking God for help and guidance. My efforts were almost always met with this painful silence. This was in stark contrast to my prayer life during the court ordeal, when I had seemed to receive just the right answers and guidance to continue another day. In every conceivable way, I was lost and could not find my way back home again.

This painful dryness of prayer began soon after my acquittal and continued for several years. Prayer became very forced and mechanical and usually just resulted in fatigue. Despite what He had done for me, I would experience anger and frustration with God. Periodically, I would be given five short consoling words that occasionally came to me out of the silence: *Michael, do you love Me?* As the painful silence once again returned, I was, thankfully, always able to say yes.

I have slowly learned that this can also be a quite natural experience following trauma and suffering. This is particularly true if the suffering was long-term. It is impossible for a soul to exit this life unscathed by this phenomenon if it chooses to accept its higher destiny.

For me, God's silence did not remain forever. Almost as if this had been a long dark night, the sun eventually rose in the morning. Looking back on this period now, however, I see that I experienced more growth in my prayer life than at any other time in our ordeal.

As the sun returned and the night lifted, I also experienced a significantly deep emotional healing from my trauma.

My paralyzing depression slowly began to lift each day. Laura was experiencing a similar result. If we choose to embrace them, the long dark nights can forever elevate our Christian life. These periods of God's silence can almost be seen as a gift for our growth. A spiritual foundation will result that will serve God, serve our souls, and serve others.

* * *

Our victory over our ordeal was overwhelmingly positive and could be considered bittersweet only upon an accounting of the worldly losses. We must never forget the final chapter. This is the essence of our Christianity. It ends in a paradox with seeming failure in the eyes of this world. The world saw God's Son as poor and abandoned upon a cross, while the angels rejoiced and untold glory awaited Him beyond the veil.

The ranks of our Christian Church are filled with those who have never received the triumphal, miraculous healings. This is okay. We have no need for the triumphal and miraculous to compel our belief; merely an unwavering faithfulness even in times of affliction. Millions of people courageously travel this path in anonymity every day. Their tremendous sacrifices and losses go unnoticed to a self-absorbed world. Laura and I joined them, and the worldly losses and the years of our life that were taken from us as a young family were and continue to be heartbreakingly tragic.

This story, however, is not complete with a sole accounting of our losses. After walking out of that courtroom, I had Laura at my side and Madison waiting for me at home. The years to follow would prove to be tough ones; however, I would gladly walk the same path today. My world suddenly became very simplified and reduced to the bare essentials of a truly successful life: an intimate and dynamic relationship with a loving God who is well pleased with my choices and a family who looks upon me with a deep sense of love and admiration. What more do any of us really need?

When our power of choice reflects God's will, we will never be promised a road to fame, fortune, and recognition in this world. These promises are not nearly big enough to reside in His world. God's plan for our lives involves promises much bigger than we could ever imagine. The essence of our Christianity saves God's greatest victories for the last chapter in His book. For my family and me, this was our experience as well.

Quell Our Internal Demons

"That I might not become too elated, a thorn in the flesh was given to me, an angel of Satan, to beat me, to keep me from being too elated. Three times I begged the Lord about this, that it might leave me, but he said to me, 'My grace is sufficient for you, for power is made perfect in weakness.'" (2 Corin 12:7–9)

We cannot know what "thorn" Paul was speaking of that tormented him so. We can be sure, however, that we will all share his experience at some point in our lives. Many times, our thorns will present themselves after some of our greatest successes and victories in life, when we should be enjoying the fruits of our efforts in tranquility. After marching through hell and slaying the dragon, we find ourselves incessantly tripped up and paralyzed by a pebble in our path. These become obstacles to our mission.

These pebbles become particularly difficult for us when they come in the form of internal conflicts and confusion. The civil wars taking place within us are sometimes tougher to fight than the external dragons we have slain in the past. Doubts, fears, lack of confidence, depression, and anger are all worthy adversaries that can surface at any time, particularly following our most admirable successes and accomplishments. Far from being elated, we seemingly become locked within mental prisons and begin to feel abandoned by God.

St. John of the Cross, a sixteenth-century mystic, wrote much about this experience, referring to it as the Dark Night. This period in the desert is God calling us closer to a new relationship with Him and a new relationship with His creation. During this time, we must listen for guidance and allow the Holy Spirit to take our prayer lives to deeper and more intimate levels. Refuse to remain attached to your old manner of prayer. The previous spiritual "sweets" were not God anyway, and He is now pulling them away, urging us, "Live for me alone."

This perceived abandonment by God causes many souls to quit and opt out of this new call as the spiritual dryness takes its toll and leads to a crisis of faith. Much additional pain comes from an attachment to the past and an unwillingness to surrender to God's new call. Sadly, many people fail to grow into the new relationship God so desperately wants to enjoy with all of us.

This is when we must plunge recklessly deeper into the darkness, meditate upon His promises, and pray for the lamp to light our steps. (Ps 119:105) Father knows best. Sometimes, the idealisms we seek are the source of our sufferings. Our gratitude for the divinity and will of God should always be for what it is, not for what we want it to be. Our old selves must be put to death as we live for God the consolation rather than the consolations of God.

The closer we get to God, the more pain we shall initially feel. As we draw closer to God in this life, the illumined light is blinding and painfully hot to our fallen human nature. We see our flesh and misery with much more clarity. Our impurities that were previously suppressed are now revealed and abhorrent to us; however, if we remain strong during our Dark Night, we ultimately become internally attuned to this light as it becomes increasingly peaceful and embracing. We know we never have to go through this misery again. God knows our pain in virtue of His Son and offers a yoke that is easy if we ask for help. Having already purified our intellects, God wants to purify our wills as well. Our souls do not advance until they are perfected. (Rev 21:27) This is the path to God that we shall all experience in this life or the next.

Our souls shall never put boundaries upon us. They simply keep expanding if we allow them to. God's nature is one of creation. When we listen with love and detachment, we expand. Many benefits await us following a complete and loving submission to the will of God, perseverance in prayer, and remaining at peace through the Dark Night. As we stumble our way through the darkness, we gain a greater knowledge of ourselves and God. Our character becomes more refined in charity, humility, submission, obedience, and virtue. As the darkness lifts and we find ourselves once again in the light, we are changed forever in union with Christ.

Once we are pardoned and healed by Christ, we must become messengers of His mercy. Jesus left the temple and went out into the marketplace. So should we. We cannot be passive any longer. We are commissioned to dominate the world for Him. By accepting His healing, we must also accept His demands. In this life we are called to work and spread His message to others, rather than follow a self-interested pursuit of pleasure and comfort. When we answer the call to our mission, we shall all get crosses and many thorns along the way. This is when the fight gets tough. However, this is also when power is made perfect in weakness.

CHAPTER TWELVE:

The Mountain Appears

"For I know the plans I have for you," declares the Lord,
"plans to prosper you and not to harm you, plans to give
you hope and a future."

Jer 29:11 (NIV)

AS I WALKED OUT OF THAT federal courtroom on August 25, 2000, after being fully acquitted by the jury, I felt like I had reached the top of the mountain. I had never felt so close to God than at that time, when I knew His will for me with a certainty, hearing His voice loudly within. I had also been witness to an avalanche of miracles with no human explanation, which lifted me up from a hopeless cause against a powerful foe, sparing my life. It was a long and tortuous climb, but I had finally reached the mountaintop; at least that's what I would have said if you had asked me on that day.

I was wrong. Far from the mountaintop, I soon discovered over the next few years that I was merely in the foothills. I know this because the true mountain has risen splendidly before me. As I look back at the impressive distance I have just climbed, I remain dwarfed before this true mountain. I now know that a far more glorious and heightened peak awaits all of us, far greater than we could ever imagine. How small-minded of me to think my foothill was my goal and destination!

Mt. Carmel is there for all of us. She is the mountain of our Christian faith. Her glorious peak is where our true nature is ultimately fulfilled and we shall finally see God face to face. This union is why we were created. The path that leads to her and begins to traverse her rocky terrain is always there for us. Nonetheless, it only appears through our free power of choice and is never forced upon us. The difficult choices of our ordeal, in union with Christ, allowed me to find the path to the mountain and become an oriented traveler once again.

During our ordeal, the clouds momentarily parted and I was given a slight glimpse of Mt. Carmel's majestic peak. All words fall short, and this glimpse beyond the veil exists only in my memory now. The clouds quickly returned, obscuring her inspiring magnificence.

Today, I continue to climb with her memory still in my mind. It is difficult to blindly travel to a destination you cannot see. The climb is often in darkness, and each step must be taken with care. Many paths beckon that can quickly lead over the precipice into oblivion. The rocky terrain causes us to stumble and fall often, leaving us battered and bruised. The pain, however, is always overcome by the vivid memory of her. Even though I cannot see her, I know she is there and I know what she will be like when I finally get there. For this reason, I pick up and continue.

Once we begin the steep climb of the Christian life, it is not possible to turn back. After glimpsing for one moment Mt. Carmel's glorious peak, we will never again be content to remain in the foothills. As we spend our remaining years ascending her peak, we discover that the higher we climb, the greater perspective we gain on the terrain below.

As we gaze down from the heights, God's fingerprint becomes increasingly revealed interwoven throughout the years of our life tapestries. This intricate pattern of wisdom cannot be seen from the valley floor at the foot of the mountain. This was the place of seemingly unceasing struggle and heartache with no apparent purpose or design. Now the view is much clearer. It takes time, sometimes years, to ascend to the point of this new transcendent perspective.

This is the reason why this chapter could not be hastily recorded. We are now closing in on nearly a decade since walking out of that federal courtroom back in 2000. The ripple effect resulting from the bold life choices we made has been permitted ample time to gain significant momentum. The time has now come to fulfill the purpose for writing this book: to offer hope by sharing what God has done in our lives and to perpetually keep the momentum of His ripple effect traveling outward and touching others.

In these past ten years, God's greatest gift to us, our power of choice, has unleashed the most powerful force on our planet: His unbridled grace. We could not have foreseen the extent of what His grace could do in all of our lives.

Despite the trauma of her early years, Madison has grown in virtue and holiness in the years that followed. She has become an inspiring model of moral leadership for others that I never was at her age. Laura and I are especially proud of the great life choices she has thus far exhibited at her young age. She has learned very well from the lessons of my nightmare and my poor initial life choices.

As a result of enduring her early childhood stress, Madison was definitely shaped by the process. One can understand how God permits us to experience these traumas to prepare us for bigger things to come. To this day, Madison still remembers that doorbell ringing on her first day of kindergarten orientation and the ensuing chaos. These events seemed to develop within her some extremely powerful character traits.

One of these traits is an incredible mental toughness. Whether excelling in a rigorous academic environment, playing through pain on the softball field, or taking an unpopular stand in the face of peer pressure, Madison continues to be the strong rock the FBI agents remarked about many years before. This is the complete opposite of myself at that age.

Madison has also developed into a person of extraordinary compassion for others. Even through the challenges and insecurities of the teenage adolescent years, Madie has chosen to consistently lead with her heart. This has exhibited in many areas, such as participating in the mission fields of Honduras, volunteering in her local community, and stepping up as a charter member of a new Pro-Life club at her school. And just like her mother, Madison has learned to stand up and fight for the underdog. She definitely learned from the best!

For a few years following our court case, we continued to receive the blessing of Father John's influence. He always enjoyed seeing our family in our first-row pew. His fiery, inspiring sermons at church sometimes brought healing tears to Laura's eyes. Along with his individual counseling, he had an uncanny knack for ascertaining the needs of his flock and then speaking directly into our hearts. He was truly gifted.

After our ordeal, Father John's spiritual gifts seemed to increase even more. His beneficiaries numbered far more than just us as the entire outside community began to transform as well. Father John's influence helped struggling ministries begin to flourish, and he began to receive much-deserved rewards and recognition far and wide. This is always bittersweet.

Father John became known as a fire-starter. When an assistant pastor begins to have such a positive influence, it will never be long before he is called to serve and reignite other communities in need. This is exactly what occurred to Father John, and Laura and I miss him very much and pray for him daily. From afar, we follow his progress as he serves a new community every two or three years. It is great to know that so many others can now share in his gifts.

Jim, our attorney, also continued to do well following our court victory. His reignited passion for law continued to grow as a result of our case. His practice became a community resource for justice for countless innocent individuals caught up in an unfair system. Just like with Father John, the community also began to bestow much-deserved awards and recognition upon Jim for his work, as well as his ensuing philanthropy for the less fortunate.

Jim would also be my conduit for periodic insight into the legal fallout from my case. After leaving the courthouse that day, Agent Hennessey and Agent Stone were never heard from again. The initial high hopes of awards, recognition, praise, and career advancement that could have been garnered from my court case never materialized for them. After what was exposed of their work and exploits in the courtroom for all to see, I would not find it surprising to see Hennessey return to his previous job in the car rental world and Stone joining him behind the counter!

U.S. Attorney Hill was another story. We did hear of his whereabouts following our case. After squandering thousands in taxpayer dollars on a corrupt indictment and full trial, he left the U.S. Attorney's office to try his hand in private practice. Apparently, Hill's personality was not suited for this endeavor. After only a few months, he retired from law altogether after meeting with zero success and even fewer clients.

Since our ordeal, the faith of our extended families has blossomed considerably. The ripple effect of grace, initiated by courageous life choices in accord with God's will, becomes apparent and seems to take on a life of its own as the years pass. Parents, brothers, sisters, nieces, nephews, cousins, aunts, uncles, friends, and countless others who were somehow associated or acquainted with our experience were touched forever as they were witness to a Creator who can create beauty out of nothingness. As the free-flowing nature of grace touches us, we, along with our families, become better in every possible way. In turn, we then become free to pass these graces on to others. The incredible growth in faith that Laura and I witnessed occurring in all of them was very exciting.

In the years since Laura and I have walked out of that courtroom, faith has become a living, breathing reality for us. Our faith has become the center of our universe, and all else must contend for a secondary place around it. For both of us, in the years following, faith has increasingly become something that must be *lived* out. In this way, we truly were changed by our ordeal.

I have been drawn to an apostolate of providing health care for the indigent and uninsured of our community. Along with my continued private practice, this takes the form of serving weekly at a clinic along with other doctors, resulting in some of the most fulfilling work I have ever done. In addition to this, I coordinate food projects for an inner-city mission and am working hard to establish a foreign mission outreach partnership with a community in Latin America. I love every bit of this work and wish it could be more. Prior to my six-year nightmare, I was always too busy or simply too self-absorbed to consider serving others in this manner. Now, my biggest concern is not having enough years left in life to give back to God all that He has given me and my family.

Increasingly, I have also started to receive speaking requests to share our story. I have met many wonderful souls in churches, schools, organizations, companies, and conferences as I share with them our inspirational story and the message of boldly using our power of choice for God. I continue to be surprised at the number of individuals who come up afterward and share stories of experiences similar to mine. They thank me for encouraging them to fight for themselves and their families.

Laura has also found herself increasingly on the path of service both in and out of our home. Shortly after our trial, she quit her job and became a full-time mom. She has relished these years with Madison without the hovering dark cloud of stress and uncertainty that blanketed us for all those years. Laura was born to be a mom. She has done a wonderful job raising Madison even through the tempestuous period of teenage hormones.

Several years after our trial, the living reality of Laura's faith expanded even further as the ripple effect of God's grace continued to push outward within our lives and the lives of others. With remarkable courage and vulnerability, Laura reached out and reconciled with her father following many decades of painful separation. Our Christian faith calls us to bury the pain of the past, and Laura did this extraordinarily well. For both of them, this emotional, tearful reunion felt as if Heaven and Earth shook under their feet upon the joyousness of the occasion.

Shortly after this incredible event, Laura began to experience some puzzling health problems. She kept this to herself for several weeks. Eventually, the uterine pains became too much. She finally told me and reluctantly made a doctor's appointment. We both feared the worst.

The nurses and doctor conducted a thorough and careful examination. The doctor then sat down beside Laura as she worriedly awaited their findings. He directed her attention to a video monitor beside her bed. "Laura, the pains you are having appear to be due to pressure on a uterine fibroid," he relayed with a perfect professional stoicism, pointing to the affected area. "If you look above this, however, you can see what is applying this pressure. It looks like you are ten or eleven weeks pregnant," he told her, smiling along with the two nurses nearby.

Tears began to well up in Laura's eyes. "Are you sure?" she asked softly.

"One hundred percent. You are going to be a mom again," the doctor said with his smile continuing.

I could not believe it when she called me on her way home. We both stared endlessly at the tiny image on the sonogram printout. In every way, this was supposed to be an impossibility, according to all of the medical experts.

"It's a miracle," we kept saying to each other.

The miracle did not stop there, however. Despite her forty-one years of age, Laura's nine months of pregnancy could not have gone any more smoothly. Her uterine pains quickly disappeared, and she began to have more energy than ever before. She felt stronger than ever, as well, walking three to five miles per day. More importantly, Laura exhibited absolutely no signs of the organ failure and gestational diabetes that had plagued her pregnancy with Madison fourteen years earlier!

We were now clearly living in a world where all things are possible. God's grace was removing barrier after barrier in our lives. One of the last imposing and formidable barriers for us had always been the impossibility of having more children. This was bolstered in our minds by the best and brightest of the medical community and their hallowed opinions and the almost sacred-like nature of the diagnosis. Despite this, God's will shall be done, and on June 20, 2008, Joshua Michael was ushered into this world.

Six weeks later, the calendar read August 9, 2008. This was the nine-year anniversary of the early morning government raid upon our home. The doorbell, the flak jackets, the assault weapons, and my arrest were always vividly triggered within my memory every year on this date. On this new day, however, things were much different.

Our family found ourselves at church that Saturday morning to celebrate the baptism of Joshua. As we held his tiny body over the massive baptismal font, the priest said those special words as we all looked down at Joshua. "Joshua, I baptize you in the name of the Father, and of the Son, and of the Holy Spirit," the priest said smiling as he thrice gently poured the small chalice of water over the top of Joshua's head.

Instead of crying, Joshua smiled the entire time. Maybe he knew more than we thought. Forevermore, August 9 will now be an enduring symbol of the marvelous works of God's grace.

* * *

My desire was to offer our story to all individuals gallantly engaging in life's struggles, heartaches, and sufferings and to those fighting to just stay afloat. Like myself for many years, you may even find yourself canvassing and imprisoned within the depths of a self-imposed pit, or hell on earth, that seemingly holds no options for escape. I recorded the message of the previous pages to simply offer a way out.

The answer resides in God's greatest gift to us, our power of choice. When we are fully employed for God's purposes and will, the walls of overwhelming obstacles and seemingly impossible situations come crashing down. For all of us, as we make God's choices, our lives and the lives of our families are forever changed and catapulted to heights previously thought unreachable. God will always provide the doorway for His dreams for us, but we must make the first move by trusting and then choosing Him.

More often than not, the choices for God's plan are not the easy choices in this life. The unwavering trust and tremendous courage required of us may only be summoned as a last resort. God understands this. When we have exhausted ourselves through human effort and have experienced little or no temporary relief, finding ourselves at an incredibly low point of human existence, the doorway just became closer. This is the beautiful grandeur of humble submission, and we now become extremely open to God's guidance and to God's ways.

Our power of choice possesses the greatest potential for impacting our future during these most painful crossroads and turning points in life. We are given the full opportunity to allow our integrity and character to shine, radiating God's glory for the world to see. The God-inspired life-changing choices one person makes amid the darkness becomes an unstoppable force of light that spills over into the lives of our families, our friends, our coworkers, our churches, our cities, and beyond. This highly contagious influenza of God's grace, ever widening and extending in its influence, subjects all matter of human circumstance to its dominion. Love binds all things. (Col 3:14)

Our power of choice is always there waiting for us. It does not guarantee immunity from the trials of life. There will always be a series of ups and downs as we ascend the glorious peak of Mt. Carmel. Rather, our power of choice merely extends an invitation to all who use this awesome gift as an instrument of God's grace.

This invitation is to a future of freedom, happiness, and truth that was always meant for us. These three absolutes are not the elusive worldly ideals chased after by a wounded humanity. The doorway to authentic freedom, happiness, and truth that our power of choice unlocks leads not to a destination but to a person.

Jesus never takes anything away from us when we walk through this doorway. He simply asks us to choose to give up something good, in order to receive something greater. Courageously trust this solitary whisper of a voice in the midst of a thousand contrary worldly voices. When we do this, we are left to forever view life in a grander way. Our world becomes a truly magical place to live, and our future with Him becomes even brighter.

Eternity will be an impartial judge of our work, clearly revealing to us how each of our choices held limitless potential for our lives and our families. We will also discover that millions of souls redemptively awaited the human choices that only we could make during our years. What will be the result from our lifetime of choices? Any lost opportunities will be tragic. As Christians, we must refuse to be wasteful stewards of any of Christ's gifts. (Jn 6:12)

About the Author

Dr. Michael J. Norman has owned a family health center offering chiropractic care and wellness programs since 1992. Since 2003, he has also served as a staff doctor at a non-profit center offering health care and life services to the indigent and un-insured of his community. In addition to his practice, Dr. Norman enjoys writing, speaking, mission outreach and completing graduate studies in Theology. He lives with his family near Dallas, Texas.

Dr. Norman is available and would welcome the opportunity to speak to your church, organization or group. He enjoys sharing the message within Unbridled Grace as well as numerous Health and Wellness topics. Dr. Norman's inspiring programs can be specifically tailored for the needs of your event. To schedule an event, please contact him at 972-394-3350 or on the web at www.UnbridledGrace.com, www.DrMichaelNorman.com or by email at DrMichaelNorman@msn.com.

Share Your Story

We all have a story to tell. Have you too experienced the most powerful force on our planet, God's Grace, become unleashed as a result of making a courageous personal choice for God? We would like you to share your story of what God has done for you, your family and your world and how it came to be through the power of choice. Inspire others who may be facing similar choices and possibly become a published author in the process in a future edition. Please submit your stories in hard copy, along with your contact information, by mail to:

Dr. Michael J. Norman
3740 N. Josey Lane, Ste. 216
Carrollton, Texas 75007

CPSIA information can be obtained at www.ICGtesting.com
Printed in the USA
LVOW13s1853140114

369254LV00004B/5/P